Entrepreneurship in youth

Farshid Aramjoo

Elahe Tushe

Nima Taheri

Entrepreneurship in youth

ISBN: 9798859350094

INTRODUCTION

Many of us want to achieve wealth and success, so what better way to experience success and wealth at a young age Entrepreneurship is one of the ways by which we can achieve wealth and success of course, in order to become an entrepreneur, we need a series of skills and characteristics. It is better to strengthen these characteristics at a young age in order to achieve success at a young age. The book you are holding is the result of the efforts of 3 entrepreneurs in the field of entrepreneurship, who by researching in this field have gathered all the features and skills that you need to have in order to become an entrepreneur at a young age.

This book shows you the possibility of entrepreneurship at a young age and teaches you the dos and don't so that you don't step on the wrong path. You may have to change some of your habits and give up your old beliefs I think that you, who are reading this book, are interested in becoming a successful entrepreneur at a young age, and you can be sure that by following a series of rules and regulations, you can become a young entrepreneur with great success. So roll up your sleeves and move forward with the utmost effort Maybe one day when you wake up in your own home, you will see life in a way that you dreamed of before

CONTENTS

Job

Job is one of the key words in economy and business. But the meaning of this word in the life of every person is much more general and vital than its meaning in the economy. Since childhood, every person dreams of having income and an exciting job that he can proudly experience as a job. In childhood, this job is more of a game and entertainment aspect that is mixed with desire, but steadily with increasing age and even away from academic education. This desire and attraction towards a job turns from desire and entertainment into a reaction to transform talent and energy and various trainings into a financial source and spiritual satisfaction and even the continuation of intellectual life.

Work Definition (Statistics Center)

Any intellectual or physical economic activity that takes place in order to earn money (cash or non-cash) and its purpose is to produce goods or provide services.

definition of worker (statistics center)

People aged 10 years and older (minimum specified age) who have worked at least one hour in the calendar week before the census week (reference week) according to the definition of work, or have temporarily left work for some reason.

The International Labor Organization (ILO) has a different definition of work and occupation that is closer to what we in society know as a job.

Definition of work (International Labor Organization)

Any activity performed by any person of any age and any gender with the aim of producing goods or providing services and benefiting himself or others is considered work. "Official or informal" and "legal or illegal" are not included in the definition of work.

Although the definition of the International Labor Organization is a little clearer than the definition of the Iranian Statistics Center, it is still useful for economists, statisticians and macroeconomic policy makers, and we need a clearer definition in the business environment. The following definition can be more understandable for a young person who just wants to enter into serious thinking about his work and career and his future.

A job is a set of:

Duties
Activities (Tasks)
Responsibilities

which is assigned to a person in the work assigned to him and in a certain environment.

What is mean by job opportunity?

A job opportunity means a job position for which a suitable person has not yet been found and hired. When a person leaves a group or a new job position is defined, it can be said that a job opportunity has arisen. So, for example, if a person wants to immigrate to another country, he usually does not look for how many job positions there are in that country. Rather, the question is "Are there enough job opportunities in the destination country?"

Or if we want to be more precise: "Are there suitable job opportunities for immigrants in the destination country?"

In terms of job opportunities, age and gender affect, but not the level of efficiency of the person defined for that job. (Of course, the work definitely includes people over 17 years old)

The nature and definition of entrepreneurship

The essence of entrepreneurship is understanding and exploiting opportunities. This is the definition that Schumpeter proposed in 1928. The meaning of opportunities is not an opportunity that you want to find and cultivate in life after completing many studies and scientific degrees. Creative and successful people know the opportunities ahead and even the future from a young age and take advantage of them, so when we talk about a successful entrepreneur, it means someone who has been creative and opportunistic since they were young.

What is entrepreneurship and who is an entrepreneur?

In our society, a person who started his own business is called an entrepreneur. Also, when we hear the word entrepreneur, we tend to attribute it to a person who started his investments. In fact, the official definition of entrepreneurship is the process of starting a business or organization to make a profit or meet social needs. We have used this term for profit or social needs to separate commercial entrepreneurship from social and charitable entrepreneurship. After defining entrepreneurship, it is time to define who an entrepreneur is and what they do.

An entrepreneur is someone who develops a method of earning income, provides the physical and human capital necessary to start a new venture, makes it operational, and is responsible for its success or failure. Note the emphasis on the phrase responsible for success or failure because the entrepreneur is different from the professional manager; This means that the entrepreneur either invests his capital from his own resources or raises capital from external sources and is therefore responsible for failure as well as the reward in case of success, while the professional manager performs the work assigned to him in consideration of payment. In other words, in addition to creating a new company, the entrepreneur is risk-taking and innovative, while the professional manager is the only executor.

Characteristics of entrepreneurs

First and foremost, we examine the skills and abilities that an entrepreneur should have regardless of gender and age; He must take initiative and come up with a change idea or a potentially new concept that can succeed in a crowded market. Note that investors usually tend to invest in ideas and concepts that they feel will generate sufficient returns for their capital and investment, and hence, the entrepreneur needs a truly innovative idea for a new investment.

Creative destruction and entrepreneurship

Often when we talk about the elimination of some companies or the success of others, as well as maintaining our leadership position in the market, we come across the term creative destruction. Creative destruction refers to the replacement of weaker products and companies with more efficient, innovative, and creative products and companies, in which the ecosystem-based capitalist market ensures that only the best survive, while others are eliminated by the goals of creative destruction. In other words, entrepreneurs with an idea for change and the skills and attributes to succeed ensure that their products, brands, and ventures take market share from existing companies that either don't create value or are simply inefficient. Therefore, this process of destroying old and ineffective ideas through new and innovative ideas is known as creative destruction, which is often done by an entrepreneur when starting a new venture.

An entrepreneur is a risk taker

We discussed entrepreneurship and the skills and characteristics needed by entrepreneurs along with how they interact in creative destruction. This does not mean that all entrepreneurs are successful; Because there is the fact that they can be victims of creative destruction; In addition, due to the lack of other attributes, the majority of new investments do not last more than a year. When investments fail, the obvious question is who is responsible for the failure and whose money is lost. The answer is that the entrepreneur invests his own money or takes capital from angel investors and venture capitalists, meaning that if the venture fails, the entrepreneur and the venture capitalists lose their money. Note that as mentioned earlier, professional staff and managers will lose their jobs unless they participate in the investment; Otherwise, their money is not at risk. This means that the entrepreneur is exposed to risk, which means that the success or failure of the company reflects on the entrepreneur.

Some famous entrepreneurs

According to this initial introduction to entrepreneurship, we can now point to famous examples of entrepreneurs who have succeeded despite low odds; Because they had the ideas of change and most importantly, the necessary qualities and skills that made them legendary. For example, Microsoft founder Bill Gates and the late Apple founder Steve Jobs were college dropouts, although their success mean that they not only had innovative ideas, but were prepared to execute on them over the long term and persevere when the going got tough. Even the founder of Facebook, Mark Zuckerberg, as well as Google's Larry Paytt and Sergey Bryan can be considered as truly revolutionary entrepreneurs. What all these legendary figures have in common is that they had a vision and a sense of mission to change the world, and with hard work, perseverance and a nurturing ecosystem, they were able to turn their ideas into reality.

The topic of entrepreneurship and teenagers

One of the best decisions parents can make is to expose their teens to real situations and challenges. Teaching entrepreneurship to teenagers can be one of the best decisions that every parent can make for their child's future at this critical age. Because understanding entrepreneurship makes teenagers aim for financial and intellectual independence in other stages of life.

The difference between a purposeful person and an aimless person

People without a purpose have to spend their whole lives so that people with a purpose reach their goals sooner. Purposeful people have a daily schedule. Difficulties and problems do not stop them and they are constantly solving challenges and issues. While the aimless people, when they face these challenges, their first solution is to abandon the destination.

Purposeful people are very persistent in the activities that they had planned in advance. Everyday events do not stop them from their daily tasks and predetermined activities, while aimless people are surprised by everyday events and are constantly changing their path.

It might be interesting for you to know that goal-oriented people remember the future and the passing of time fondly, but those who do not have a specific goal are constantly worried about the passing of time and wasting their energy. Many people in society think that entrepreneurship education for teenagers only leads to business education and earning money! But the truth is that entrepreneurial skills will not be useful for a person if they are not accompanied by personal development.

Worthy entrepreneurs of tomorrow should improve their entrepreneurial qualities along with business training so that these trainings will bring them an increase in income.

Benefits of entrepreneurship in teenagers

There are countless benefits of entrepreneurship, but these benefits are especially true for young people who have not yet entered the labor market. Mastering entrepreneurial skills can be helpful in many areas of your life as a teenager.

Entrepreneurship can be a challenging but very rewarding journey, and in addition to gaining impressive knowledge and skills, aspiring entrepreneurs gain the confidence to tackle real-world problems and pursue their dreams. This is an ideal way for young people to discover their interests and talents and learn how to use these gifts to their advantage in their future careers.

In addition, entrepreneurship helps teenagers think creatively, develop analytical and problem-solving skills, and look for ways to learn, evaluate, and improve their work. Entrepreneurship is truly the best preparation for young people with any career aspirations, from art to finance.

Independent thinking

One skill often overlooked in schools is independent thinking. Schools rely heavily on memorizing information and knowing the correct answer for tests. However, in the real world, there is not always one right answer, and sometimes conventional wisdom is not the best way to solve a problem. Employers know this and colleges know this and are looking for employees who demonstrate the ability to think independently and provide unique solutions to common problems. Therefore, it is important that a smart teenager does not limit his information only in textbooks and school sayings. This is exactly what entrepreneurship can help in developing the thinking of a teenager. To succeed as an entrepreneur, you need a competitive advantage or differentiation that doesn't come from doing things like everyone else. The show will provide a unique perspective to college recruiters and admissions, and the development of these skills will accelerate a teenager's success in life and career.

Financial freedom in entrepreneurship

It would be irresponsible and incorrect to say that every entrepreneur gets rich from his business. However, the truth is that entrepreneurship is a way that allows people to create unlimited income potential. Most jobs have limited salaries, and even with an increase in annual bonuses, there is a limit on employees, and the speed of their income increase is also limited. Entrepreneurship is just the opposite and there is no cover for it. There is no limit to how much money you can make or how fast you can grow your income as an entrepreneur, allowing for financial freedom. Not only can entrepreneurs achieve whatever level of income they seek, but they can also create businesses that are passive, recurring, or freelance. Even when the founder is on vacation.

So what more do we want than limitless potential and freedom in life for teenagers to do what they want and pursue their dreams without financial worries?

Lifelong skills for success

Entrepreneurial skills are not only useful in business. The skills that entrepreneurs develop are almost transferable to other areas of a person's life and career. Entrepreneurs learn and master everything from time management to delegation, persistence to critical analysis and more. Of course, these are just a few of the skills that are transferred to many other aspects of their lives.

Starting a teenager's business

Teens who aspire to become entrepreneurs should break their goals down into small chunks, such as first identifying a problem or getting a certain number of friends to pitch in for a startup.

Starting work at this time in life allows teens to work hard at every step of the goal setting and goal-achieving process, and when they're looking for bigger goals like getting into college or even running for president, they know where to start.

In addition, it is important for teenagers to ask their parents for sympathy and help and to understand that there are not limited options for their future. For teenagers, whose world and future are theirs, there is no reason to limit their dreams or potential, and it is their responsibility to have open discussions about the future with their peer group, parents, and teachers.

Cultivating and strengthening the entrepreneurial mind

Becoming a successful entrepreneur, beyond knowing how to manage finances, requires learning other skills such as creativity, leadership ability, and strength. These are not the same skills needed to learn mathematics and are not learned as such. Instead, developing an entrepreneurial mindset requires learning both inside and outside the classroom, and drawing on your own experiences and those of others helps a lot. So there are several methods that you can use.

1- To strengthen the entrepreneurial mind, listen to experienced coaches.

One of the most practical things you can do to strengthen your entrepreneurial mindset is to find a mentor and listen to his experiences. Some of the most successful people in the world, such as Mark Zuckerberg, attribute their success to the experiences they shared with their mentors.

2- Read as much as you can.

In addition to trainers, you can gain knowledge from published books and articles to strengthen your entrepreneurial mindset. People who write about their experiences and share them with the world want you to learn from their mistakes and successes, providing real-world stories that you can apply to your investing. For example, most successful CEOs indicated that they read at least a few hours a week

3- Participate in entrepreneurial events and conferences.

If you want to be better at what you do, what should you do to develop an entrepreneurial mindset?

Meet other entrepreneurial minds at events such as trade shows, conferences, webinars, and more. Such events are great networking opportunities. Having connections in industries related to your business will most likely bring you success. Your goal in attending these conferences is to make professional connections that will help you in the future.

4- Look for new challenges.

The most important skill an entrepreneur can have is problem solving. To develop your entrepreneurial mindset, you need to learn how to think quickly, assess situations from different angles, and come up with creative solutions that no one has ever done before. To develop such skills, you need to pursue challenging situations and think critically. For example, you must learn to accept feedback and criticism, listen seriously to the thoughts and ideas of others, and decide to focus on results and solutions.

5- Think about your vision every day.

You want to be an entrepreneur; Because you have an idea and a clear vision. Think positively about your future vision every day to remind yourself why you are developing these skills and putting yourself through such stressful situations.

6- Motivate yourself if needed.

Even many successful people have said that they used affirmations to inspire themselves and strengthen the entrepreneurial mind:

• I have enough experience and I have enough knowledge to do this.

• I am prepared enough and mature enough to do this.

• I have enough courage to do this.

7- Keep your promises

One way to differentiate yourself from the competition is to over deliver. This habit will not only improve your reputation, but also foster better customer relationships and boost marketing in your favor.

8- Try every part of the business.

While you are an entrepreneur, you have a lot to do to foster an entrepreneurial mindset. However, when your business grows and you have employees to help you, you may forget how difficult these responsibilities are. So try to work with your employees in different roles to see what their job is like. This will help you become aware of their issues and provide opportunities for collaboration and bonding as a team.

9- Practice discipline.

Being a successful entrepreneur requires discipline. In order to strengthen your entrepreneurial mind, you must be careful about wasting time both in your professional life and in your personal life. Limit the amount of time you spend on social media, make sure you get enough sleep and eat balanced meals, schedule time for exercise and study, and reduce distractions.

10- Listen more than talk.

Always listen more. As they say, there is a reason we have two ears but only one mouth. So it's better to focus on listening to what other people are saying (not just verbally, but through body language and other social cues).

11- Help other people.

In the field of sharing business experiences and strengthening the entrepreneurial mind, helping others is one of the most practical things we can do. Helping others with entrepreneurship can teach you a lot about your own business. Being an entrepreneur is not just about running a business. It requires a new way of thinking and how can you strengthen your entrepreneurial mind?

Characteristics of successful people compared to others

Warren Buffett is successful in investing and building long-term businesses. Bill Gates was successful in building a software empire that has changed the way computers are used. Gandhi succeeded in leading India to independence. Success comes in many ways and forms. The interesting thing is that most successful people have very similar characteristics. In fact, the characteristics of successful people have similarities that can inspire us.

Knowing the characteristics of successful people will help you to cultivate these characteristics in yourself and turn these characteristics into useful habits in your life. If you don't like what you are experiencing today, you need to change your reaction to events because your experience today is the result of your choices in the past. Have you ever wondered why successful people have a different lifestyle than us?

Some characteristics of successful people

Target
Perhaps the most important and the first characteristic of successful people is having a goal. Define vision and purpose. Successful people constantly seek clarity in their lives. They know what they want and follow their dreams. Ambiguous desires and opinions lead to ambiguous results. It is this sense of direction that gives them the staying power to achieve their goals and dreams.

Expertise and excellence

No matter what they pursue, they become the best in their field. They pursue their mastery and understand that money is a by-product of their desired and proposed values.

Focus

People who experience success know how to focus. They know they can't do everything. Therefore, they focus on the activities that give them the most motivation to achieve their goals. They don't believe in addiction to multitasking and they know that the fastest way to do things is to do things at once and correctly.

Positive attitude and perseverance

Another characteristic of successful people is a positive attitude and perseverance. Successful people have realistic optimism. Because no matter what the outcome, they believe that success is inevitable for them. They believe that, like a child learning to walk, they must first act and then adjust their performance according to the feedback they get. This positive attitude allows them to persevere and persevere when things are not going well.

flexibility

Most of the successful people have started with a different business and later achieved success in another business. (Example: Steve Jobs started with computers, then moved on to animation and succeeded with the iPod.) The world is always changing. Successful people adapt to changes in all aspects of life.

Stop blaming others

Believe that your problems are about you, not your parents or spouse. In addition, understand that no one is responsible for your life but yourself, so try to find the best solution with the right mindset and don't look for excuses to make others feel guilty. It really doesn't matter how much you blame and blame others, because none of it will change you.

If you want to be among the 10% of successful people, you should stop blaming others and take full responsibility for your life.

Focus only on challenges that you are capable of solving

Sometimes we humans get involved in solving challenges that we are not only unable to solve, but by getting involved, we will also make the situation worse. According to the characteristics of successful people, in order to achieve success, you have to focus on an issue that is under your control and you can solve it with your skills. You may have to take risks and jeopardize your position to solve these challenges, but in any case, whatever happens, you are responsible for it and others.

Choose your success strategies wisely

As you know, achieving success is not an easy task, in other words, achieving what 90% of people in society are unable to do is called success. Your strategy to achieve the goal you set must be smart, measurable and realistic, otherwise you cannot expect progress. What sets you apart from 90% of people is your strategy along the way to success.

Always be steadfast in your path

To become a successful person, you need a lot of time and effort, so it is not reasonable to expect that you will achieve success in a day or a week. On the way to success, you must be so resistant to become a dynamic, innovative and active person that nothing will stop you from reaching your goal.

You may sometimes encounter obstacles along the way, but these obstacles are part of the path to success. Successful people see challenges as opportunities, if you want to be one of these people, you should not give up when problems arise and stop trying. In fact, another characteristic of successful people is persistence and follow-up. Persistence is the only thing that will keep you on track to achieve your goals.

Believe that no success comes easy

The human brain naturally waits for immediate results, so most people believe that they can achieve success by working hard for 10 days or a month, but believe me, as you have seen in the characteristics of successful people, no success comes easily.

Behind the curtain of every success is the unceasing effort of a person who is not disappointed and remains steadfast in his path despite all the difficulties. Along the way, you become a new person with different skills, personality, and mindset, so you shouldn't expect these 10-day traits to change in you. Maybe now you ask yourself how long it takes to be successful? In fact, achieving the desires and success in each profession is different and depends on various factors.

Avoid negativity

When others see your efforts at work, by changing the situation, they may constantly fill your ears with negativity or blame you for every little thing, but in order to become a successful person, you should not listen to them. Pay attention to the characteristics of successful people and ignore the words and criticisms of other people and be busy with your work, after a while you will see that they will stop their negativity.

Entrepreneurial skills

A key question on the minds of many people interested in entrepreneurship is whether they have what it takes to start and grow a business, and if they don't have these requirements, how can they get them? Undoubtedly, every work needs its own requirements, and without meeting these requirements, the start of that work either fails or remains half-finished due to the deficits in the raw materials needed for it. In the case of an entrepreneur who accepts a very high risk of failure and any mistake, even a small one, can make the entrepreneur and his investor face a terrible failure, having all these requirements is more necessary than ever and will be unavoidable. In this article, with some of the most important entrepreneurial skills you will need to succeed in business.

Entrepreneurial skills framework

Before getting acquainted with entrepreneurial skills, we should know that although these skills are diverse and significant in terms of number, they can be divided into several general categories. This division, which we call the Entrepreneurial Skills Framework, is a comprehensive guide of capabilities and skills that are needed at different levels of idea and business development, especially in startup teams. Based on this template, entrepreneurial skills are included in one of the following categories:

• Necessary skills: Founders of a start-up business need a minimum level of skills that, if they do not have them, they will fail in the very early stages of entrepreneurship. These skills can be called essential skills. For example, a cautious and risk-free person cannot consider himself an entrepreneur. Entrepreneurship requires a minimum spirit of risk-taking and risk-taking, and without it, one cannot step on the path of commercializing an idea.

• Useful skills: These skills are very important for a company. But if the founders do not have these skills or are not competent in these skills, they can still compensate for this deficiency through training or hiring specialists. For example, although knowing the methods of securing capital or the principles of business negotiations are very important, you may not know anything about them when you start a company. Studying educational texts, attending specialized courses and hiring a full-time consultant or employee familiar with these fields can solve your problem in the short term.

• Startup Skills: These skills are the core business skills that will be needed for the growth and development of all companies. These skills, like useful skills, can be learned and developed through training or preferably through hiring the right people during the business expansion process. Of course, it should be noted that some of these skills are more important, especially at the beginning of starting a business. For example, at the beginning of the activities, when there is a serious lack of resources, the need to choose the right people is very important, and this is where the issue of team building skills is seriously raised. Make sure you're tapping into top talent in technical fields. These people will be the future managers of your business, and for that reason, they should have a vision and vision as big as yours, and at the same time, know technology and its development very well.

Sectoral skills: These skills depend on the industry in which you are active. A construction company needs technical skills in the construction industry and a start-up active in artificial intelligence needs software and artificial intelligence experts.

One of the most important points is that according to the statistics and studies, most startup development programs and their support focus almost entirely on startup skills and often ignore essential or useful skills. In your planning to complete and improve entrepreneurial skills, try to consider all the dimensions and aspects introduced above. For the success of a start-up business, both necessary and useful skills are needed, as well as startup and technical skills.

What are the most important entrepreneurial skills?

If you ask an entrepreneur or startup founder what is the most important skill needed to succeed in business, they will probably mention things like risk-taking, planning, the ability to manage employees, and even the ability to attract capital and manage expenses. However, it should be noted that every startup activist looks at this issue from his own point of view and may even state what caused him to fail or stop as the most important skill. Entrepreneurial skills are all important and neglecting any of them can have many consequences for a start-up business. In the following, some of these entrepreneurial skills and habits will be mentioned:

1- Ability to manage money:

It is very simple; If you can't manage your money, you'll never manage a business. Do you know where your money is spent every month? Does your income and expenses add up? If the answer to these questions is "no", then you will also have problems managing the budget of a business.

2- The ability to increase money:

The biggest challenge facing a startup is the limitation of financial resources. What ideas do you have for attracting capital? What do you do if you don't have enough money in life? Imagine for a moment that you have a small idea in mind and you went to your rich friend (as a potential investor), what would you say to convince him? Do you create enough attraction that he wants you to continue or does he stop you at the very beginning? This situation has a very real and everyday appearance in startup businesses. If you don't think you can handle it, put the idea of starting a business out of your head.

3- The ability to reduce stress:

Stress and worry should not be underestimated. Startup entrepreneurship means unforeseen situations and numerous failures. It is natural that stress and worry will always be with you. What if the prototype doesn't work? What if the meeting with the investor does not go well? What if they don't buy my product? And thousands of "what ifs". If you allow yourself to become helpless when challenged, you will struggle as an entrepreneur. Learning how to use stress to move forward is very important. Master yourself and start the winding path of entrepreneurship by relying on your motivation and effort.

4- The ability to be productive:

This is a very important issue; However, there is no one-size-fits-all way to be productive and productive for all people and all situations. Try to learn your own method and use it to open seemingly blind and unsolvable knots.

5- The ability to find an entrepreneur friend:

Jim Rohn, a famous American entrepreneur, says: "You are the average of the five people you spend the most time with." So what do you want to be? Increase your chances of success by finding entrepreneurial friends who understand your problems and concerns more and can help solve them.

6- The ability to recognize weaknesses and strengths:

As a business owner, you don't need to be great at everything. However, you need to know what you are strong and weak at. Evaluating this issue will give you more knowledge and confidence in making decisions, choosing partners, hiring employees, etc.

7- The ability to hire efficient people:

Recruiting is one of the simplest, most obvious, yet most important skills any entrepreneur should have. Having great people on your team gives you access to new strengths and, as a result, new opportunities ahead. You should also create a favorable organizational culture that attracts others to you. At the beginning of their career, Apple or Tesla were not big companies in the sense of today. But they created an atmosphere where many inventors, idea makers and experts are interested in working in these companies.

You should note that hiring the right people is very necessary to achieve the ambitious vision you have in mind.

8- The ability to train new employees:

When you hire new people, a skills and behavioral training process ensures that they know what to do and what not to do in the future. This work will help you to move your company in the right direction and the defined vision, increase the level of commitment of competent employees and provide the ground for moving forward.

9- The ability to manage employees:

Suppose that you have identified and attracted the right people and given them the necessary training; However, if you can't manage them well, you won't get the desired result. At the beginning of your career and right when your business is growing, you are the direct manager of everyone, so you have to be efficient. If you are not a management major, learn how to motivate, inspire and develop new employees by spending enough time and study.

10- The ability to perform "SEO" activities at the initial levels:

In the beginning, you have to do what all companies do: "market the business". With that said, are you familiar with digital marketing and search engine optimization at the basic levels? If not, familiarize yourself with these before starting a business.

11- The ability to communicate and network through social networks:

Along with site SEO, social networks also play a key role in the marketing strategy of any company. Not only should you be familiar with all the available platforms, but you should also be equipped with the best strategies to introduce your startup and personal brand in each of these social networks. It is obvious that the space of different networks, such as Instagram and LinkedIn, is extremely different and you should adopt different content strategies for each of them.

12- The ability to focus on customers:

Honestly, you wouldn't have a business without customers. Note that all your products and services are focused on the real needs of the customer. If you don't know what these needs are, do some research and even ask the potential customers themselves, so you can provide excellent and acceptable customer service.

13- Ability to sell:

It is very important for customers to know that you are with them. However, haggling over the price is what causes many entrepreneurs to face difficulties in the process of offering and selling their product or service. If you express concern in this field and think that you will not be able to achieve significant success in the field of selling a product (either a product, a service or even doing a project), attend sales techniques training workshops to learn this very necessary skill.

14- The ability to identify new trends:

Businesses move quickly; Therefore, you should understand the changes that are made in the industry and your business environment as soon as possible. If your startup is based on advanced technologies, considering the short life cycle of technology and the possibility of the emergence of new technologies, always monitor the market, changes and developments in the world of technology and the emergence of new startups and developments related to your technology. Being up-to-date is the key to your success.

15- The ability to cope with failure:

There is no clear and straightforward business plan to reach the market. In a better sense, there is no straight path to success and it is very important that you know how to deal with the ups and downs along the way. Remember that every successful person you see has failed many times before becoming successful. Failure is not your goal, it is not a stopping point, it is simply a point on the road to success that you must pass whether you like it or not.

16- Desire to improve the world:

Most businesses are established to make a profit and gain wealth; But behind all the financial dreams, there is also a spiritual motivation in the minds of entrepreneurs. The best and most lasting motivation for entrepreneurship is to create a positive change in the world. When you focus your business and success on that spiritual priority, you will prepare yourself to solve any problem (no matter how big) and achieve your goal.

Entrepreneurial mental skills

In the previous section, you learned about some important entrepreneurial skills. The above skills are mainly among useful or startup skills. However, there are also some entrepreneurial mental skills that you should always keep in mind as a business leader. These essential habits and skills act as an instinctive habit in all successful entrepreneurs and bring success with them. The seven characteristics of effective entrepreneurs that form a winning mindset are:

1- The dreamer's mentality:

Successful entrepreneurs spend a lot of time thinking, creating and imagining. Being innovative comes naturally to all of us if we get into the habit of enjoying the process of continuous discovery. The most powerful asset of a successful entrepreneur is his power of visualization. The most effective entrepreneurs have a special courage to dream and turn their dreams into reality. Outstanding entrepreneurs see no limits to their creativity, success and money making. They also have a positive and permanent impact on others and involve themselves in new experiences.

2- Waking up early:

Most successful entrepreneurs are early risers. They support the belief that "be smart to be smart". They start their day by imagining what they want to achieve and talking about the certainty of success in their mind. Of course, many entrepreneurs also start their day with some kind of physical activity so that the blood is pumped to all parts of the body and their mind is alert and dynamic.

3- Programmed mind:

One of the easiest methods that entrepreneurs use to increase their efficiency is planning. They put responsibilities first and fun second. Successful entrepreneurs understand the value of getting out and spending time with people. This is not simply because of the human interaction and sense of belonging or even fun, but because spending time with others reduces stress and increases innovation. When responsibilities come first, this prioritization and planning helps entrepreneurs enjoy their free time and not worry about unfulfilled responsibilities during the day.

4- Respect the power of sleep:

Successful entrepreneurs understand the importance of sleep. The more sleep you have, the more alert you will be and the more emotionally and mentally dynamic you will be. Contrary to the existing idea about successful entrepreneurs who are always working and suffer from lack of sleep, lack of sleep causes an increase in momentary reactions and a decrease in tolerance against helplessness and can itself cause other continuous lack of sleep. This cycle is very terrifying and if irregular sleep patterns continue and are not addressed, efficiency and success become impossible.

5- Simplicity:

Simplicity is the secret weapon of successful entrepreneurs to increase their efficiency. They mostly obsessively choose a routine and simple life. This simple life helps them avoid work pressures that are sometimes beyond what logic can overcome. You are most efficient and productive when stress does not cause helplessness and despair. So be simple and cope with work pressure with this simplicity. Even great heroes need time off and peace sometimes, so give yourself that regular break by simplifying your life.

6- Flexibility:

Sufficient flexibility to change course and not insist on a previous opinion can increase the probability of success. It enhances your flexibility, learning, growth and training.

7- Curiosity:

One of the most important characteristics of a creative entrepreneur is curiosity. They happily spend endless hours doing what they love. They are looking for new information about everything, including their life and work field, and they have made it a habit. This curiosity makes them ask questions and find ideas for their next steps.

Finally, don't let this list scare you or discourage you. Being an entrepreneur is a big and difficult job, but it has its own thrills and joys. All the skills mentioned above can be learned, so if you are lacking in one of these skills, try to learn it and know that your ultimate success depends on it.

Economic and social effects of entrepreneurship

People have many physical needs. In general, they need food, clothing, shelter, air and water. In addition, they need other things such as transportation, paper, pens, books, umbrellas, tools and utensils, shoes, fuel, medicine, etc.

The people of a society rely on each other to provide the products and services they need. The more the society grows, the more specialized and clearer the role of people. It is difficult for each person to meet their needs alone. For example, a local farmer can produce rice, chicken, and vegetables for himself, but he cannot make clothes, glasses, and medicine. In the city, an active lawyer is able to provide valuable legal services but depends on the products and services of others for electricity, transportation, food, and housing.

The need for goods or services is an economic situation. When people need something, they want and are willing to pay money to meet their needs. In general, the ability of individuals to provide the type of goods and services that others need, at the right time and place and at the right price, is called entrepreneurship.

When entrepreneurship is accepted as a job by many members of a society, that society develops rapidly. The following items, which are among the benefits of entrepreneurship, explain why an entrepreneurial society develops.

1- Entrepreneurship creates employment

When entrepreneurs start a new business, they need at least one or two hired employees to organize their work. Some people hire hundreds of people. According to a report, in the third quarter of 1984, half of the 19.7 million people (about 9.85 million people) employed in the Philippines were engaged in non-agricultural enterprises. About one million of them have been employed in manufacturing factories.

When the entrepreneurial activity of a society slows down, the unemployment rate of that society increases. For example, in 1984, at the height of the economic crisis, at least 2,212 business establishments stopped working, and as a result, at least 93,886 people lost their jobs.

It was also estimated that between the months of January and October 1984, there were only 210 jobs for every ten thousand workers in Manila, and about 221 people out of every ten thousand workers lost their jobs due to the reduction of entrepreneurship and related activities. Every society wants the employment of all its competent people and its workforce. When people are employed, they are able to provide for their family's needs in terms of nutrition, housing, healthcare, and education, and they help the government a lot by paying income tax.

2-Entrepreneurship improves the quality of life

Entrepreneurs are constantly inventing new products and services. They are also looking for ways to produce these goods and services more efficiently. Such innovative efforts lead to the production of better machines and more effective production systems. Entrepreneurial commitments lead to permanent improvement of living standards. Promoting new products and performing required services makes life easier and simpler. For example, cooking has been transformed by entrepreneurs. Today, we cook with new devices such as pressure cookers, microwave ovens, rice cookers and slow cookers.

Housewives do their work just by pointing a button or turning a screw. Wood stoves, washing clothes by hand, going to the market every day and charcoal irons are meaningless. Telephone, telegraph and telex and post services have made communication faster and cheaper. Agricultural production is also mechanized in the same way, so that instead of using humans and animals, different machines are used in wheat cultivation, harvesting, milling and drying. The death rate has been significantly reduced and the average human life has increased with the help of modern medical methods. All these improvements cause what we call "quality of life".

3-Entrepreneurship causes proportional distribution of income and calms social anxieties.

Entrepreneurs are always searching, identifying or creating raw materials necessary to produce services and goods. In their opinion, almost nothing is useless. Therefore, they are the ones who usually see economic factors, raw materials and other resources in virgin areas. Entrepreneurs help to improve and develop the country by establishing institutions in these areas

When large parts of the society remain deprived, social tensions (which lead to migration to urban areas, resulting in overcrowding and a threat of revolution and opposition movements) are created.

Creating work on a large scale in the society prevents the formation of a small prosperous group who are few and become richer day by day through their work. If the work of these small groups is not monitored, they monopolize certain products and easily impose the price of these goods and services on others. With more entrepreneurs in the same field, they monitor each other and balance each other

When income is distributed proportionally, entrepreneurship flourishes and people have more money to buy the products and goods they need and give more profit to entrepreneurs. They can even invest in their own work and increase the supply of entrepreneurs.

An income that is proportionally distributed means that the poor are less. Eradication of poverty helps to solve social problems, such as youth delinquency and malnutrition.

4- Entrepreneurship makes use of resources and their activation for huge national productivity.

Our country will develop faster economically if its resources are used well. For example, we have many iron ore mines that can be used for the production of spare parts for cars and machines. The establishment of an iron smelting factory not only leads to the exploitation of raw materials to feed local industries, but also leads to foreign exchange income and time saving for the country and no need for imports. Entrepreneurship also creates a way to optimally use family financial resources and personal savings, which otherwise may be spent on ineffective purposes (such as gambling) or luxuries (such as buying imported items).

5- Entrepreneurship brings social benefits through the government.

With the revenues that the government collects through taxes, customs duties, and licensing of entrepreneurs (without considering the taxes paid by the workers of these entrepreneurs), it can invest in various projects, such as building roads and bridges, medical and educational services and facilities, maintaining peace and tranquility, and other things.

(Taken from the book: Entrepreneurship and the age of technology in the third millennium)

What is creativity and what is its importance?

Definition of creativity: You may have heard the word creativity dozens and hundreds of times, without thinking about what it is. In this article, we want to define creativity in a very simple language and see what creativity is and what it includes.

If we want to talk about the literal meaning of creativity, the word creativity comes from creating. So creativity means creation! In other words and more precisely, it can be said that creativity is the ability to make or create something new. This new thing can be a new way to solve a problem, a new way to do a certain process or a new device to do some things easily.

But as you know, creativity is a term of human sciences. On the other hand, we know that humanities words and terms usually do not have a specific and unique definition. Therefore, it is not far from the expectation that creativity, like other terms and concepts of humanities, does not have a specific, precise and unique definition. For this reason, each of the experts have considered a certain aspect of creativity and presented their definition based on that.

The concept of creativity

So that if we list these definitions, it will reach dozens. Therefore, instead of looking for a complete and actually comprehensive definition for this word, we should try to understand its meaning. To fully understand the concept of creativity, it is necessary to review a large number of definitions.

Creativity means the ability to produce multiple, new and appropriate ideas and solutions to solve issues and problems

This definition of creativity, while being simple, also tells its important features. This definition consists of several parts:

1. There is an issue or a problem that we want to solve.

2. We generate a lot of ideas to solve it.

3. We try to generate ideas that are new (not previously presented for such a problem).

4. Production ideas should be suitable for solving the desired problem and it is possible to solve the problem by choosing one or more of the best ideas

Effective factors in the growth of creativity

First, we can ask this question: Is it possible to cultivate creativity? Torranc conducted a research that formed the hypothesis of this question. Based on this research, Torrance concludes that children can be taught a set of principles that allow them to express a large number of opinions, and opinions that are much better than if they had no training at all.

Therefore, there is doubt that creativity can be cultivated. Psychologists have accepted this belief for a long time that any talent can be trained and nurtured through practice.

Rogers considers the existence of conditions necessary for the cultivation of creativity. He has stated them under the title of "internal conditions of creation" as follows:

1- Psychological safety

This stage can be divided into three interconnected processes:

A) Acceptance of the individual as an unconditional value. When we treat someone in a way that shows that they are valued in their rights and in their self-expression - regardless of their current circumstances or behavior - we are cultivating creativity.

b) Providing an environment where there is no external evaluation. When our judgments about ourselves are not based on external standards, we are cultivating creativity; Where a person finds himself in a space where he is not evaluated and measured by external standards. Such an atmosphere is immensely liberating and provides creativity.

c) Empathic understanding: Empathic understanding along with the two mentioned items provides the goal of psychological safety and this is the foundation for cultivating creativity.

2- Psychological freedom

Creativity is nurtured when we allow a person full symbolic unfoldment. Psychological freedom allows one to think, feel and be the deepest part of oneself. This fosters perceptions of concepts and meanings that are part of creativity.

Some other ways to foster creativity include: brainstorming, solving puzzles and tables, hobbies and fine arts, writing as a creative exercise, practicing creative problem solving, and reading. As Bacon, an English philosopher and writer of the 16th century, stated, studying makes a person perfect and nourishes the power of imagination, but in order to get the most out of studying, we must choose suitable subjects for studying.

Patterns of cultivating creativity

to predict

Many times we are unaware of certain assumptions or we don't want to accept that these assumptions may gradually guide our behavior and thoughts without our awareness. One way to clarify these hypotheses is the exercise of getting people to make predictions, which is a kind of thought experiment.

Looking for criticism from others

Another way to spot false assumptions is to ask others to critique our ideas. Many people avoid this. Some accept it and some get defensive when faced with it.

Analyze issues in detail

The goal is to break down our ideas into their component parts and thus free ourselves from various limiting assumptions. This strategy focuses on paying attention to actions and elements that are not usually associated with objects. For example, in relation to the various uses of a piece of brick, we can mention features such as color, weight, heaviness, shape, and the fact that it has pores and does not transmit electricity.

Use of allegory

This also facilitates creative thinking. Allegory has played a key role in the evolution of science and technology; Like Gutenberg's invention of printing, which was based on simulation.

Using the group situation to increase the generation of creative

ideas

One of the most important features of such meetings is that the subjects must adapt to the suggestions with a completely friendly and open attitude. In such meetings, sharp ideas are encouraged.

Stop working on the problem for a while and then come back to it

This is the same action that makes people sometimes feel that after working on a problem for a while and not succeeding, their thinking stops. It's not just mental fatigue. The person leaves work; Because the same old answers keep coming to his mind. Hence, he needs his mind to be broken. In this interval, he may sleep, read a novel, travel, or do anything else.

Trying to communicate in order to spread creative ideas, you have to communicate ideas. This can be done in writing; Because the written language remains over time and can be considered with a more severe evaluation. On the other hand, making ideas available to others gives us the opportunity to revisit them and evaluate them minutely. Evaluation makes us define our ideas more clearly and specifically. In the case of creativity, a model for teaching in the classroom is provided. This model includes three dimensions: subjects, teaching methods and divergent and productive thinking skills. This model fills the gap between cognitive and affective learning. Among the styles presented in the range of subjects, the following can be mentioned: the use of contrasts, the use of parables, paying attention to the deficiencies in knowledge, strengthening thinking about possibilities and possibilities, using stimulating questions using the list of attributes method, strengthening innovative thinking, searching design, paying attention to the importance of interpretation, etc.

In the book Teaching Creativity Through Metaphor, Sanders and Sanders emphasize that in order to cultivate creativity, children and teenagers should be given the possibility of divergent thinking and should be warned against doing stereotyped activities. These researchers, like many others, point to the difference in the functioning of the right and left brain and believe that the left hemisphere is generally responsible for focused thinking. They point out that the right part of the brain produces, controls and manages those activities that are in the category of divergent thinking. These people believe that the prevailing education system in all countries only cultivates the left part of the brain. One of the ways to cultivate creativity is to increase self-confidence. As self-confidence increases, so does creativity.

Personality characteristics of creative people

Because of the importance of innovative, creative and creative people in the development of societies, it is important to know their personality traits. In this context, we must first ask some questions:

1) What characteristics make these people different from other people?

2) What factors influence the development of such characteristics?

3) Does creativity cause the emergence of certain characteristics in creative people or can the owners of these characteristics be creative? There is no definitive answer to this question, but some believe that they are necessary and necessary for each other in both aspects.

Before deducing various findings, we mention the results of Torrance's study on creativity and scientific talent.

Torrance concludes that teachers favor children who have high IQ but are weak in creativity. According to this study, a creative child (example) is defined as:

He wanders everywhere in school, he enjoys learning (and not necessarily in school), he is imaginative and intuitive, flexible, inquisitive and sensitive to issues.

The relationship between creativity and personality traits can be studied since the time of Plato. He prescribed the selection of talented children in the book of Republic.

The most famous comparative research on the relationship between individual characteristics and creativity belongs to Terman. Through self-report tests and ratings of parents and teachers, Terman showed that creative teenagers attribute higher than average psychosocial adjustment to themselves.

Based on the research of Vallach, Dallas, and Gaier (1970), it was found that creativity is related to personality traits and, to a lesser extent, to some traits that seem consistent and long-term.

Creative teenagers have the following characteristics:

Capability-flexibility-sensitivity-tolerance-sense of responsibility-sense of empathy-independence-positive self-concept-need for social contacts-interest in progress.

Secrets of teenage creativity

Adolescence and its happy, sweet and stressful and exciting moments are full of memories that may have an impact on us forever. One of the most important topics that teenagers should be given the opportunity to grow and nurture is "creativity". This work should be done first by parents and then by teachers and in other educational environments, especially schools. Cultivating creativity is a very serious issue that if not taken care of, may cause serious damage to a person's future and creativity. But how can you help the creativity of teenagers to grow and develop more?

Effective factors in cultivating creativity

One of the most important and primary factors in the growth of creativity is the correct parenting methods, which, if combined with authoritative parenting, will definitely lead to good results.

Another important factor in creating creativity in teenagers is the way teachers are trained and the relationship between home and school, as well as establishing proper communication between parents and teachers; Also, the participation of the teenager in the extracurricular activities, the degree of sincerity of the teachers is very effective in creating this matter.

Also, the wishes of teenagers should be respected; For example, when choosing a field of study to enter the university, it is necessary to pay attention to his interests. Some teenagers like to get to know the working environment and even get to know the job market environment and gain experience.

Formation of adolescent personality

In fact, it can be said that a teenager's personality is formed through failure, success or taking responsibility in the educational environment of the school. Of course, school can also be effective in the development and formation of a teenager's personality in another way. It is true that the important role of parents as the first educators of children cannot be ignored. But it must be said that little by little, as teenagers enter the educational environment, school teachers play an important role in this field, along with parents.

Among these, one of the most important reasons for the important role of educational environments; The role of teenagers' peers is very important at this age. Of course, teachers also play an important role in this regard.

Why is creativity so important for entrepreneurs?

In today's economic world, entrepreneurship is the main factor of economic growth. Entrepreneurs try to create more opportunities in the industry, provide more employment options and ultimately have a positive impact on per capita income, income generation, lifestyle, etc.

Developing a new position through creativity and entrepreneurship

In entrepreneurship, it is important to explore new aspects of traditional business. This can be in the form of changing the way the product or service is produced or how they are presented to the user. All these areas can create a balance that has great potential in business.

Entrepreneurship and creativity - how are they related?

We now assess that entrepreneurs can attribute their success to creativity. But what exactly shows the connection between entrepreneurship and creativity?

Entrepreneurs connect the creative mind and the business. In today's world, due to globalization and excessive industrialization, products are produced and exported to international markets. As a result, there is easier access to any product, everywhere. The consumer has access to different types of products with different types and quality. So what does an entrepreneur do in the market with his products? How to separate the product from the rest?

The creative mind answers all these questions. Creativity helps us think about how to improve existing business practices. A brand may be very basic and popular among consumers, but there is always something that can be different from the rest at its best. The creative mind is like an artist creating new and exciting patterns on the canvas. Creativity can be achieved with unimaginable ideas and innovation in existing ways.

Creativity is simply the ability to imagine. Imagination allows everyone to achieve something they have never tried before. In business terms, imagination just means "think different". Using imagination, an entrepreneur can set aside practical norms and think of something creative and innovative.

However, a creative mind must have entrepreneurial skills to bring these creative ideas to life in a business environment. An entrepreneur evaluates the needs of how to implement the idea by evaluating the available resources against the required resources, how to create a new company and how to manage it. He builds business models that can initially support and implement innovative ideas. And it also provides the "science" aspect of how artistic creativity comes to life. Thus, it bridges the gap between creativity and traditional business approach. There are indicators that show the creative thinking of a successful entrepreneur. Creativity brings the entrepreneur to the competitive stage, but how do you evaluate whether they are creative enough or not?

The following characteristics are characteristic of a creative entrepreneur:

1. An entrepreneur only follows rules and principles and adds value to the organization and has more power for customers.
2. An entrepreneur tests initial ideas. The second step is to learn

through experience and the third step is to implement what has been learned.

3. An entrepreneur has a high risk-taking power and is not afraid of failure and is always interested to be tested in new companies.

4. The entrepreneur knows the new ideas of each region directly or indirectly related to the company.

5. An entrepreneur is not afraid to enter new markets beyond the industry. This opens up a range of opportunities to shape new markets.

6. An entrepreneur creates a new product for an existing service.

7. An entrepreneur does not shy away from understanding new ideas, generating creative ideas quickly, regardless of who is in front of him.

8. The entrepreneur shares an idea and waits for feedback that improves the idea.

These indicators show that entrepreneurship and creativity go hand in hand. Entrepreneurs are flexible and seek to improve their creativity more than they search.

Creativity must be organized.

Despite all the flexibility in doing new things, creativity needs a framework for successful implementation. However, too much structure spoils the whole essence of the process. It is important to take a careful approach before it becomes too difficult. Researchers say that creativity is used in two different ways: convergent and divergent. A convergent approach focuses and searches for a single solution using available information. However, divergent thinking works to generate many creative ideas in different directions.

Creative thinking is not the only skill required for entrepreneurship.

The debate that has so far led us to think that entrepreneurship is deeply rooted in certain basic skills: generating new ideas and having the ability to take risks. However, you should know that this is not the only skill required to successfully implement an idea. Creating an idea may be easy but succeeding in it may be difficult. What makes an entrepreneur successful? Why do some people recognize the opportunities around them and others don't understand them? Do they have different genetics? Do they have a different perspective on things?

There may not be definitive answers to these questions, but researchers have suggested some areas that the entrepreneur should have expertise in.

(source (cleverism)

The role of the manager in fostering creativity

The role of management in collections where creativity and innovation is essential and the main factor is very important and sensitive because management can create, promote and encourage the ability and talent of creativity and innovation in people, or his behavior and performance can prevent this vital thing. The art of the creative manager is to use the creativity of others and find creative minds. The creative manager must create a space where he can be creative and stimulate the people of the organization to be creative as well, and this space is a space that is far from everyday work and somehow delegates authority so that everyone can solve their own problems.

In order for people in the organization to think, an environment must be created in which ideas and thoughts can be expressed. One of the very important and attractive methods of cultivating human personality, as well as creativity and innovation, and even social development is consultation, and without a doubt, people who are good at consulting have more wisdom and thought, and those who are not good at it do not benefit from this privilege. A creative organization depends a lot on the self-control of its employees. Self-control shows itself in wanting and wanting to provide initiative and creativity.

Managers can influence all three components of creativity namely expertise, creative thinking skills and motivation. But the fact is that influencing the first two components is much more difficult and time-consuming than motivation. Intrinsic motivation can be significantly increased even with minor changes in the organization's environment. This does not mean that managers should forget to improve expertise and creative thinking skills. But when it comes to prioritizing action, they need to know that effective actions on internal motivation will bring more immediate results.

Innovation

Innovation means creativity that has been manifested and reached the stage of action, in other words, innovation means realized creative thought; Innovation is the provision of new products, processes and services to the market; Innovation is the application of mental abilities to create a new thought or concept.

What does creativity include?

Some people believe that creativity is innate, others believe that anyone can become creative with training. In the second perspective, creativity can be seen as a four-stage process composed of perception, cultivation, inspiration and innovation. Perception is the way of seeing things. Being creative means seeing things from a unique angle. In other words, an employee may see solutions to a problem in a way that others cannot. Going from perception to reality doesn't happen instantly anyway. Instead, thoughts go through the process of cultivation. Sometimes employees need to reflect on their thoughts. This does not mean no activity, but at this stage employees have to pour the massive data that they have stored, retrieved, studied and reshaped into something new. It is normal for years to pass through this stage.

In the creative process, inspiration is the moment when all your previous efforts come to fruition. Although inspiration leads to prosperity, the work of creativity is not over. Creativity requires an innovative effort. Innovation means taking that inspiration and turning it into a useful product-service or way of doing something. This saying is attributed to Edison that "Creativity is one percent inspiration and 99 percent perspiration," in other words, 99 percent of innovation is testing, evaluating, and re-testing those things that have been received by inspiration. It is usually at this stage that a person makes others more aware and involved in what they have been working on.

How do structural variables affect innovation?

Based on extensive research, we can express three propositions according to the structural variables. First, mechanistic structures have a positive effect on innovation because their work specialization is lower, they have fewer rules, and lack of concentration in them is more than mechanistic structures. They also increase the flexibility, adaptability, and fertility that make it easier to adopt innovations. Second, easy access to abundant resources is a key factor in innovation. Abundance of resources gives managers the ability to afford innovation and accept failure. Finally, communication between units helps to break possible barriers to innovation by accelerating the interaction of organizational lines. Of course, none of these three variables can exist unless senior managers are committed to these three factors.

How does organizational culture affect innovation?

Innovative organizations have a similar culture. They encourage experimentation. They reward both successes and failures. They gain experience from mistakes. An innovative culture has the following seven characteristics:

1- Acceptance of ambiguity
2- Patience in impractical matters
3- Few external controls
4- Risk tolerance
5- Patience in encounters
6- Emphasis on results rather than means
7- Emphasis on open system

Ideation and its techniques

What is ideation?

Ideation in English: Ideas is actually a kind of mental idea that is presented in the conditions of lack and need, and as a result, it is an effective step for growth and progress from the current situation. With ideation, you can draw the situation in a completely different way and create a new development in the relevant field.

Remember, for pure ideation, you must strengthen your mind in any situation; Even in absolutely critical conditions, because many ideas are the result of lack of resources. In fact, if you have everything, there is no room left for ideas.

If you look at the history of inventions, you will see that inventors really started working because of shortages. So let's strengthen Edison's thinking in us right now so that a foundation is provided for future generations. Now the question arises for you, how do we really develop ideas?

The answer to this question is very simple and we should pay attention to the fact that we do not need to put pressure on ourselves to come up with ideas, but with sufficient self-confidence and knowledge of our surroundings, we create conditions for our brains to blossom the bud of our idea.

idea creation

Ideation to solve a problem or provide one of the business requirements can be a good starting point for many businesses. Companies usually identify pain well. But more important than diagnosing the problem is providing a platform for ideation for pain treatment. Ideas are not only solutions to problems, and apart from therapy, they are also used in two other areas: competency-based and customer needs assessment.

In the competency-based field, ideation can be used to increase the company's capabilities. In this type of ideation, the organization seeks to create new services and products or new markets for existing services and products.

Choosing an idea

Choosing the best ideas starts much earlier than the ideation process. This is where determining the criteria against which ideas are measured, who is responsible for evaluating them, and how key ideas are presented to internal teams for further evaluation and implementation becomes important. We usually start the good selection process by using labels and tags to transform ideas into meaningful categories. For this purpose, we can categorize products: mobile, laptop, tablet (tag); In the next step, we consider more details and "tag" the features or characteristics of the product: for example, lightness, long-life battery, portability... or we go to features such as operating system, screen, etc. In the next step, we prioritize the ideas using these labels and tags. Categories and tagging should act like a filter and only bring the best ideas to the implementation stage.

Implementation of the idea

Success in the implementation process depends on the organization's ability to select the best ideas and act on them. In addition, the organization must have a regular work flow, so that the employees of the organization are well aware of their role in the different stages of the ideation process. If an organization wants to start idea generation, designing a suitable process for idea generation (that is, clearly specifying roles and responsibilities) will be very important. People who are chosen for different roles should be ready to accept new ideas; Ideas that are not necessarily created within the organization. It may even be possible to reward these people based on their performance in implementing new approaches.

Effective techniques in ideation.

list making

Making a list is a completely analytical method in which, by identifying the strengths, we list the various features of the offered product or service. For example, in order to understand how we can make a product better, we separate its parts, note the physical characteristics of each part, and examine all the functions of each part to see how a change in each of these has a positive or negative effect on the product's performance.

Questioning assumptions

In most businesses, there are unwritten but effective principles that everyone refers to to get things done. Unfortunately, no one realizes that questioning these assumptions at every step means opening the door to new ideas and possibilities!

"Participants need to frame the creative challenge," Mattimore(1999) says of questioning assumptions. Then they should prepare 20 to 30 assumptions (whether correct or incorrect). In the next step, they should choose some assumptions from among them and use them as a stimulus to create a new idea or start thinking.

Partnership efforts

As the title suggests, in the collaborative technique, two or more people work together to achieve a specific goal. Designers usually act in this way and give wings to their creative ideas in collaboration with others and a group of colleagues.

You can determine which technique you should use by considering the type of problem, the attitude of managers and employees to the issue, and the available facilities. In any case, don't forget, the more free and "natural" the ideation process is followed, the better the idea will be.

Vigilance or environmental sensitivity

Identifying and choosing the right opportunities for new businesses is one of the most important abilities of a successful entrepreneur (Stevenson et al., 1985). Therefore, examining the recognition and development of opportunities is an essential part of entrepreneurship research (Venkataraman, 1997).

Entrepreneurs identify business opportunities to create and transfer value to the intended business stakeholders. Although the elements of opportunities may be "identified", opportunities are made rather than found (Ardisvili et al., 2003). Careful search and sensitivity to market needs, as well as the ability to recognize suboptimal use of resources, help the entrepreneur develop an opportunity (this may or may not lead to a business). But the development of an opportunity also requires the creative action of entrepreneurs. In this way, "Opportunity Development[2]" and not just "Opportunity Recognition" should be considered because the recognized opportunity does not lead to actual business without the "Development" action (Ardisvili et al., 2003).

The needs of the environment and the market or unused resources are recognized only by a certain number of people. One of the reasons for these differences is the heterogeneity of people's sensitivity to environmental opportunities to create and transfer new values.

Some people are so sensitive to the needs or problems of the environment that they continuously understand the possibility of developing new products (solutions) in any environment where they are present (Endsley, 1995). These people easily find potential opportunities by observing phenomena. This sensitivity to problems or possibilities does not necessarily lead to the creation of ideas for solving problems; In fact, anyone who is an expert in questioning cannot necessarily provide good answers.

Other people may be particularly sensitive to unused or suboptimal resources. However, even recognizing these resources, these people are not necessarily able to define specific uses or users to create value. Inventors, scientists, or other individuals may develop ideas for new products and services regardless of market acceptance or commercial feasibility of the new invention or technology.

One of the ways that increase people's sensitivity and alertness is information asymmetry and prior knowledge. People are sensitive to information that is related to their previous information (Van Hippel, 1994). Based on this, Shin (1999) states that entrepreneurs recognize opportunities because prior knowledge makes them recognize the value of new information. Based on the opinion of Austrian school economists who say that entrepreneurship exists due to the asymmetry of information between different actors (Hayek, 1945), Shin states that each entrepreneur recognizes only the opportunities that are related to his previous knowledge. In the three-stage research of opportunity recognition processes, Shin (1999), tests and confirms several hypotheses, which are summarized as follows:

• Not every entrepreneurial opportunity is obvious to all potential entrepreneurs (because people do not have the same information at the same time; Kirzner, 1997).

• Each person's specific prior knowledge leads to the creation of a "knowledge corridor" that allows him and not others to recognize certain opportunities (Hayek, 1945; Ronstad, 1988).

Three basic aspects of prior knowledge that are important to the entrepreneurial diagnosis process are: prior knowledge of the market, prior knowledge of ways to serve the market, and prior knowledge of customer issues.

Entrepreneurial consciousness

An introduction to theories related to entrepreneurship

Regarding entrepreneurship, many hypotheses have been presented so far, which in many cases have major differences, but almost all of these theories have addressed 3 common features: the nature of entrepreneurial opportunities, the nature of entrepreneurial people, and the nature of the decision-making contexts in which entrepreneurs operate. All entrepreneurship theories use these three characteristics, however, this does not mean that they have the same assumptions. (Alvarez, 2005)

In general, the two theories of opportunity discovery and creation have been more popular. Although these two theories have different and even conflicting assumptions, according to Alvazer (2005), they can complement each other. Discovery theory, which is consistent with Kirzner's assumptions, is based on the assumptions that opportunities are objective, individuals are unique, and entrepreneurs have a high risk tolerance. Meanwhile, creation theory, which is related to Schumpeter's view, considers opportunities as subjective, entrepreneurs as ordinary people, and conditions as uncertainty.

In the theory of discovery, Kirzner describes these unique people as people who are different from others in recognizing opportunities and have entrepreneurial awareness. (Alvarez, 2005 and Shin, 2003) In fact, he considers the entrepreneurial element in human action in the form of being aware of information. Craig (2006), in his article, adds ownership of information to it, and argues that entrepreneurs do not necessarily need to be ignorant of information, but they must have ownership of it, that is, know how and where to recruit people who have access to information. (Craig, 2006) In fact, the basic concept of Kirzner's entrepreneurship theory is awareness. Consciousness leads people to discover opportunities that fulfill human needs. The role of entrepreneurs is due to their awareness of the opportunities that have remained unknown until now. It is through awareness that they will be able to identify and exploit situations in which they can sell what they bought cheaply at a higher price.

Although Schumpeter introduces entrepreneurs as ordinary people in his theory, Kirzner, in an article he published in 1999 comparing entrepreneurs from his perspective and Schumpeter's, reexamines Schumpeter's perspective on entrepreneurs, and states that from this point of view, entrepreneurs are also conscious people. He considers this awareness from this point of view, courage, self-confidence, creativity and innovative abilities. (Kizner, 1999)

Opportunities and search for information

Discovering opportunities, like other human activities, requires knowledge and ignorance of problems. (Yu, 2001) Kirzner, (1973) states that unawareness of opportunities is related to two types of knowledge: intentionally learned knowledge, and unintentionally learned knowledge. The first type of knowledge can be obtained through deliberate search, which includes technological knowledge, and knowing what to buy, where, and how to sell. The second type of knowledge will be acquired only through daily life experience. In deliberate knowledge learning, a person compares the cost-opportunity of subsequent searches. But in many cases, even when the company is deliberately looking for opportunities, it does not find them. This is why many companies set up research and development units to identify profitable opportunities, but fail. (Yu, 2001)

Yu (2001) also states in his article that in deliberate information seeking, it is assumed that agents know enough about this domain of knowledge, that they know what kind of information they need and where to look for it. In fact, they need some kind of framework or paradigm to guide them. Yu concludes that when we do not have information about a subject, it is impossible to search for it, let alone estimate the cost-opportunity of related searches.

Rogers (1983) also agrees with this argument, stating that much learning and search originates from dissatisfaction with current information. It is this dissatisfaction that makes us search for better and more information. This prior information is not the result of deliberate search, but is formed from the accumulation of our everyday experiences. (Rogers, 1983)

Maria Miniti (2004) in the article Entrepreneurial Awareness and Asymmetric Information in the Spin-Glass Model examines the relative role of awareness and asymmetric information in entrepreneurial decisions. In this article, a model is presented in which a person decides to become an entrepreneur based on his awareness or information available in his surroundings. The simulations of this model are used to show the dynamics of the decision-making process. Based on the obtained results, more conscious agents are more likely to show entrepreneurial behavior. However, if the information is evenly distributed, the number of entrepreneurs is very small even when the entrepreneurial practices have high consciousness. On the other hand, if the information is not evenly distributed, it has been shown that entrepreneurship increases and is geographically concentrated. In addition, entrepreneurship has been identified as a path-dependent phenomenon. As a result, this model states that the institutional and political situations are more guiding entrepreneurship than other situations and it implicitly means that probably the short-term policies that aim to promote entrepreneurship are not effective. Entrepreneurial opportunities exist when information is asymmetrically distributed among individuals. In this case, smart people turn the advantages of information into profitable opportunities. Asymmetric information creates conditions that are necessary to create an entrepreneurial culture.

The emphasis on information in economic theories is not new. In fact, the works presented by Hayek and Kirzner put information at the heart of entrepreneurship and market dynamics.

In addition, people are different from each other because their environment equips them with different information. Entrepreneurship is possible only when an entrepreneur can identify and follow a profitable opportunity. Also, the discovery of opportunities and the next levels of entrepreneurial activities necessarily depend on the existence of asymmetric information. In entrepreneurship, activities depend on trial and error, and entrepreneurship and the subsequent results of entrepreneurial activities are governed by search activities and information processes.

The formation of entrepreneurial consciousness

According to Yu (2001), not much is known about what constitutes entrepreneurial consciousness.

An existing view is that when people are faced with problems, their entrepreneurial consciousness increases and as a result they start to innovate. This view is called problem solving. In other words, most people seem to wake up when they face a crisis or a rapid change in external conditions. Yu (1997), in his book, compared the state of entrepreneurship in America and Hong Kong, and concluded that both of these countries can be recognized as entrepreneurial economies, but since the people of Hong Kong are facing more political and economic problems, this has made these people need to be aware of opportunities in order to survive. But we see that the American people have always been aware of opportunities. It can be concluded that external conflicting conditions can lead to entrepreneurial awareness. In fact, the assumption that people only react to external environmental stimuli is not always true.

Another point of view that Kirzner puts forward is that the internal motivations are caused by the individual interests of people, which lead to the expansion of consciousness in entrepreneurs. This view is called entrepreneurial selective attention.

In addition to the mentioned reasons, it seems that the most important factor in increasing entrepreneurial awareness is competition with oneself. Khalil (1997) considers it a competition between the future self and the past self, which originates from the desire of the current self to test his abilities. The passion of entrepreneurs is business. They want to realize their vision. This passion often overrides the desire to make a profit. It is because of this self-challenge that entrepreneurs often create uncertainty for themselves and the market.

However, entrepreneurs are usually not aware that they have this "source of self-consciousness"; Or in other words, they don't know that they have such a resource. (Kirzner, 1979)

Previous research on entrepreneurial consciousness

There have been 3 schools of thought about entrepreneurial consciousness:
1. Austrian economic landscape
2. Behavioral perspective

3. Cognitive perspective

Austrian economic perspective

According to Kirzner (1973), awareness is like an "antenna" that enables one to detect gaps in the market for which there are few external indications. Entrepreneurs always choose a high place because from there the signals of market opportunities can be better received by these antennas. (Gilad et al., 1988) Entrepreneurs can "smell" such opportunities. This special sense is always active and through it they can select unseen aspects of the environment. So, even if the entrepreneur's current business is profitable, he still keeps himself alert.

Entrepreneurial opportunities involve creating new products, services, or raw materials, as well as organizing ways to sell outputs for more than the cost of producing them. Opportunities are objective and should only be discovered, identified and observed by entrepreneurs. So we can't search for something we don't know exists or not. According to Kirzner, opportunity discovery is different from "successful prospecting." Astute people discover opportunities with wonder, because they realize that there was something in the world of reality that they did not realize until now. (Unintentional Discovery) What is discovered are opportunities "that attract the attention of only the most alert people without knowing what to look for." (Tang, 2007)

Of course, Kirzner's consciousness is by no means a "mere accident". Rather, it is something between deliberate search and sheer luck. Or in other words, discovery through intuition. Luck favors the prepared. The entrepreneurial process occurs when individuals, aware of the misallocation of resources, realize that resources are not in their original place, acquire those resources, recombine them, and sell them for more than they cost.

A behavioral view of consciousness

This view emphasizes the "information seeking" behaviors of entrepreneurs. This information seeking may be informal and 'unplanned', but it is ongoing and helps build one's knowledge base. In other words, how entrepreneurs do things differently can explain why they are more likely to spot opportunities than others. According to this view, the behavior of "gathering and accumulating information" is the main characteristic of consciousness.

Cognitive view of consciousness

This view considers consciousness as a distinct cognitive process. These researches seek to find out how the market environment is shown in the entrepreneur's mind and are the mental models of entrepreneurs different from non-entrepreneurs? The work that has been done so far in this field is mostly theoretical. Entrepreneurs with this skill habitually form a pattern to recognize signals or changes regardless of whether they seem appropriate at the time. Consciousness, as a cognitive ability and skill, is placed in a spectrum that should be conceptualized and measured accordingly. (Tang, 2007)

There are four views on this continuum:

1. Assessing: People who recognize the imbalance and are interested in making changes in their patterns.
2. Discounting: People who are able to recognize signals and clues of imbalance in the market, but tend to interpret them in a way that reduces their effect.
3. Dismissing: People who recognize signals and clues but choose to ignore them.
4. uninterested: people who are not aware of market opportunities at all.

Yu (2001), in his research, concluded that when entrepreneurs' interpretive frameworks are disrupted, they respond differently. Interpretive framework is: a device that receives external information and organizes itself in the form of patterns. This framework helps one identify and solve problems, and identify opportunities. When people have new experiences or acquire new external information, their interpretive framework pattern is disrupted. Some people consider this new incident as an obstacle or deviation and reject it, while others may easily ignore it because it makes no sense to them. But, entrepreneurs look another way and "see outside the box." So, they either modify the existing classifications, or add another classification to their framework, to give it meaning through "re-creation". (Yu, 2001)

Tang's information processor approach

Tang (2007), in his doctoral dissertation, takes the information processor approach and reconceptualizes it.

The information processor approach specifies what happens during the acquisition, storage, modification, and use of information. Applying this approach to entrepreneurial consciousness allows us to integrate the three existing perspectives. First, the information processor approach examines how people search for information (then gather information in consciousness). This approach then determines how people react to this newly acquired information (the transformation of information into consciousness). Finally, the information processing approach explains why some people, and not others, are able to set aside unimportant information and store and use important information in identifying profitable business opportunities (the dimension of conscious information selection).

The author defines entrepreneurial awareness as an individual ability to collect, transfer and select information that leads to potential business opportunities and claims that this definition includes all three approaches and their components. Kaish & Gilad (1991) emphasize the importance of searching for new information, which includes the receiver dimension of information gathering. Gaglio & Katz (2001) show that the ability to receive, understand and interpret the environment comes from breaking the existing tool-goal framework, and this is the basis for the dimension of information transformation. Kirzner (1985) emphasizes the unique ability of entrepreneurs to perceive profitable opportunities that have been overlooked by others, which constitutes the dimension of information selection. These three dimensions of awareness play a different but complementary role in explaining how awareness affects opportunity discovery. In order to better understand each of the dimensions of awareness and the mutual relationship between these dimensions, an existing model related to the process of opportunity discovery, which is based on the psychological theory of creativity, has been used. One of the models introduces opportunity discovery as a step-by-step process that includes gathering, latent and insight. The main feature of the model is that opportunity discovery is not limited to a specific moment, but rather an iterative process in which insights are pondered, new information is collected and transferred, and knowledge is created over time. (Tang, 2007)

Preparation and collection of information

The preparation phase deals with the storage of information that an entrepreneur collects for the process of opportunity discovery. Prior knowledge is linked to a person's specific information about a specific subject and provides him with the ability to identify specific opportunities. Although every type of knowledge has an explicit component, personal knowledge is often tacit in nature. The information gathering and vigilance dimension asserts that entrepreneurs gradually become accustomed to assessing and monitoring their environment in order to recognize and gather information that is critical to opportunity creation. This dimension is consistent with the behavioral approach to consciousness and assumes that information-seeking behavior is the main component of consciousness.

Latency and combination of information

Incubation refers to the part of the opportunity recognition process where entrepreneurs think about a particular idea or problem. This stage is not the same as problem solving, but means that choices and possibilities are considered. It is during this time that new relationships are likely to be formed. Although information storage is important, it alone cannot be sufficient to describe the latent stage. The ability to transform information in sensory storage, by combining scattered information and creating inherent models from them, promotes the latent stage. This dimension is related to the cognitive approach of consciousness, according to which conscious people tend to act differently and modify their interpretive framework of existing means-goals. If the possession of information can be considered passive, the transfer or regularization of knowledge for profit is a progressive and entrepreneurial process.

Insights and information selection

Insight refers to a momentary experience and is the point at which a complete answer or fundamental solution unexpectedly reveals itself. This revelation is the result of the collapse of the existing interpretive framework. upon arrival While insight may appear to occur without thorough (detailed) analysis, these astute entrepreneurs may nevertheless fully and continuously process the information available to them. In other words, they are well prepared in collecting and transmitting information.

Sham or frost business

In the Oxford English Dictionary, we read about the meaning of acumen: the ability to make quick and good decisions. However, experts believe that business sense is a collection of knowledge, skills and experiences that are transferred to us in the form of strategic companions in our organization (Garguillo et al., 2006). He categorizes this knowledge, skills, and experience into three main areas: financial skills, partnership skills, and communication skills. Also, Rome (2006) believes that business intelligence is a concept that is related to a person's knowledge and ability to make profitable decisions and is placed in the field of organizational learning and development circles. It is worth noting that today this term is used as a tool to strengthen financial and leadership skills in business (Summerfield, 2008). These words somehow convey the same meaning and concept of entrepreneurial awareness.

It seems that there is still no single definition of this word, but it can be looked at from different perspectives. For example, this term can be examined from the perspective of human resource management. In this area, business intelligence is related to business intelligence through the ability to interpret data (Tyndall et al. 2009) and this can be a good clue to its connection with the topic of entrepreneurial intelligence. Limited research shows that part of this ability is achieved through innate behavioral characteristics (Leadership Development Institute Report, Press, 2008), but most of it can be learned.

This term has recently attracted a lot of attention from researchers. For example, (Prince, 20009) emphasizes that powerful economic trends are moving towards increasing the importance of business philosophy in perspectives that deal with the development of leadership skills. He describes these trends as follows:
- Slow movement of the world economy
- Lack of basic goods in the world
- Developing countries that are not familiar with the traditional views of leadership
- Environmental cost-benefit issues

Sham and Frost business should be considered in the field of intellectual and knowledge assets of business (Ganz, 1998). Raising it is also in the area of knowledge responsible (CKO). In general, the duty of such a position in the organization is to turn knowledge into profit by leveraging the company's intellectual assets. One of the characteristics of such a person is business acumen. This person must be aware of the company's performance and have the necessary knowledge.

Decision making process for entrepreneurs

The entrepreneurial decision-making process will be effective in determining the direction of the organization and achieving the set goals and perspectives. Things like being familiar with the risks and conscious risk-taking, as well as the commitment to execute and implement the decisions made, significantly help to complete this process.

Getting to know the stages of the entrepreneurial decision process

As mentioned, the entrepreneurial decision-making process is very important. In an organization, this process can be seen in various dimensions and forms. However, all of these decisions are made with the same goal of improving results and improving business conditions. The most common current approach in entrepreneurs' decision-making includes the following steps:

1- Identification of problems and shortcomings

Identifying problems and shortcomings can be considered the most important step in the entrepreneurial decision-making process. This means getting to know the current situation in detail and recognizing its differences with organizational perspectives. To do this, you must first define the goals and prospects well, and then examine the current problems and obstacles to achieving the overall goals.

2- Analysis of problems

It is better to list all the problems and obstacles and prioritize them according to their impact on the organization's achievements. In this way, you can analyze each of the mentioned issues based on their urgency and decide how to fix them.

3- Explaining the possible solutions and identifying the factors causing the problem

In the process of entrepreneurial decision-making and in order to solve existing problems, you will probably come across a wide range of possible solutions. Naturally, explaining the solution will require investigating the causes of problems and obstacles. Without considering the causes and effective factors in creating obstacles, an entrepreneur can never provide a comprehensive solution. In this case, the proposed solutions will be temporary. Therefore, identifying the effective reasons for creating problems is one of the most important decision-making steps for entrepreneurs.

4- Analysis and review of proposed solutions

At this stage, you need to list and analyze all the proposed solutions, both the best and the worst. Doing this clearly outlines the angles of each solution and identifies their strengths and weaknesses. This will be effective in achieving a comprehensive and practical solution.

5- Choosing the best solution

After going through all the mentioned steps, it will be possible to choose the best solution. Therefore, according to the analyzes and reviews, you can choose the most suitable option and take steps to solve the organization's problems.

6- Execution and implementation

Undoubtedly, the importance of the entrepreneurial decision-making process is in the implementation of decisions and the examination of the results obtained from them. Otherwise, the mentioned process will be incomplete and invalid.

Factors affecting entrepreneurs' decisions

Entrepreneurs' decision-making and problem-solving are continuous processes that require evaluating situations and problems, considering all options, and continuous follow-up. Sometimes, this process has to happen in a very short period of time. That is, it is necessary to select and implement the best possible option within a few seconds. In other cases, the process can go on for weeks or months. In general, the factors influencing entrepreneurs' decisions can be listed as follows:

- Unity and coalition
- Insight and insight
- Commitment and responsibility
- Recognizing risks and risk taking
- Adherence to ethics

Unity and coalition

Unity and coalition are one of the most important elements that affect the entrepreneurial decision-making process. This means solidarity with employees and organizational teams to achieve a common goal and requires the ability to benefit from their opinions and ideas. However, in some cases, shared purpose may replace decision making! For example, shareholders or employees of an organization may band together and impose a certain decision on the board of directors. In fact, it is necessary for managers to ensure the benefits of alliance with other team members and reduce its adverse effects.

Insight and insight

Insight comes from an inner belief and mental structure. Sometimes, the decisions of entrepreneurs and managers are based on the experiences gained over many years and following different paths. This inner sense may help these people to make some decisions without considering the logical sequence of things.

Commitment and responsibility

Among other factors affecting the entrepreneurial decision-making process, commitment and responsibility can be mentioned. This feature brings practical actions based on the decisions made and responsible follow-up of its consequences.

Recognizing risks and risk taking

Recognizing risks and taking risks is one of the important features that accelerates the decision-making process at critical times. Some managers are extremely cautious and conservative and make their decisions only based on logical patterns. Of course, caution is a condition of reason and prevents heavy losses. However, in some cases, risk-taking can be effective in choosing more creative options. This is provided that the managers are familiar with the existing risks and threats and know how to deal with them.

Adherence to ethics

Ethics means the personal beliefs of people and their interpretation of the rightness or wrongness of behavior. The entrepreneurial decision-making process should be aimed at providing benefits and advancing the goals of the organization. In some cases, group goals may conflict with managers' personal interests and disrupt the decision-making process. This is where ethics become important. Basically, managers should examine the advantages and disadvantages of each option and analyze the positive and negative effects of their decisions in a larger perspective and considering the public interest. Obviously, this will affect the decision-making process of entrepreneurs.

Problems in the decision making process

Decision-making is one of the most important organizational processes and its adoption, especially in a group, is associated with many problems. Among these, the following can be mentioned:

• Team decision-making is time-consuming and takes a significant amount of time.

• In team decisions, people may compromise with each other and limit their choice to the satisfaction of a particular person or group without considering the public interest and final results.

• Many participants in the decision-making process may not have enough experience and knowledge and only comment based on their subjective opinion. This is despite the fact that entrepreneurs' decisions are mainly based on knowledge, experiences and attention to the long-term interests of the organization.

• Some decisions may be biased and unfair and only serve the interests of a particular person or group.

• The instability of environmental factors and the uncontrollability of some of them may make decision making difficult. At the same time, sudden changes and developments in social, political or economic structures will affect the decision-making process. In such cases, managers are forced to change their decisions and course of action depending on the requirements of the time.

3 approaches to start entrepreneurship

In general, there are three common approaches to start entrepreneurship:

1. Do the things you are good at: Think about the things you have done for others in the past. Is it possible to sell the skills and expertise of your past work in the form of a product or service to the client?

2. Do what everyone else is doing: Find out about other businesses that interest you. Once you have identified one of them well, just imitate it and persevere.

3. Solve a problem in society: Is there a gap in the market? Does the service or product you want to market already exist? If you decide

to do this, you should increase your knowledge in that area before spending and starting work.

Where should we start to start our own entrepreneurship or business?

1. Research: Before doing anything, you must first identify and choose your business idea and then take action to make it a reality. The first step is to research to see how valid your business idea is in today's market. You must be asking how and from where we should understand and do this validation? The answer is that for a small business to be successful, it must have one of these three conditions: solve a problem, satisfy a need, offer something that the market wants, and after you find one of these three conditions in your business idea, you should do research.

2. Plan: Planning in entrepreneurship will help you achieve success faster. In order to turn your business idea into reality, you need a plan or outline. A comprehensive and complete business planning will guide your business from the very beginning to the end of its growth, success and fruition, and this issue is essential for all new businesses. If you are considering getting help from an investor or financial institution as a financial support for your business idea, having a long-term and detailed planning with full details seems very necessary. If you also have no intention, a general and simple one-page planning can give you a clearer picture of what you hope to achieve.

3. Financial planning and management: Your personal life and business life as an entrepreneur are connected to each other. You are the first investor of your own business, so having an accurate understanding of your personal finances and the ability to manage them is the first step you must take well before attracting capital. You must know well the type of business in which you intend to be an entrepreneur and know how much capital you need to start and continue working. If you are considering a business with a high level of technology, you must have strong financial resources from the beginning (either invest personally or refer to accelerators related to that field and after convincing them to attract capital) or if the business you are considering is a business related to the public life of the people, you will need a small amount of capital to start. However,

no matter how small your business is, it needs some initial investment to cover its costs. Of course, until your business comes to fruition and is profitable for you, you have to pay the cost of the first months from your own pocket. Write on a sheet of paper all the start-up costs and estimate them, such as the cost of getting the necessary permits, providing the necessary equipment and supplies, insurance costs, business registration costs, space rental costs, advertising costs, production and resource supply costs, employee salaries, your own income and profit, and whatever you anticipate. These are the initial investments that you will need and you should anticipate the provision and management of these costs for at least 12 months. (online economy)

Entrepreneurial management

Entrepreneurial management is a scientific field that seeks new ideas for success in the market with strategies based on risk and innovation. It is also a university course that aims to train students with creative skills to meet the needs of the market today. Entrepreneurship is the process of establishing a business (company) based on a new thought and idea. Now, in the global arena, creative and innovative people as entrepreneurs have become the source of great changes in the field of production and services. Even large global companies turn to entrepreneurs to solve their problems. The wheels of economic development move with the development of entrepreneurship. With their creativity and innovation, entrepreneurial people have transformed the events and processes of economic and social activities of societies and brought growth and progress. The emergence of the entrepreneurial university and the significant growth of innovative companies (startups) are some of the practical effects of this issue.

Today's advanced society owes its development to people who were able to turn their dreams and creative ideas into reality, had the spirit of independence to explore new situations, and had enough courage to fight against conventional and established methods. These agents of change have had a personality and a spirit that is called "entrepreneurship" today. Entrepreneurship has both a theoretical dimension and a practical dimension, which can be aimed at training entrepreneurs with different educational methods. Due to the fact that a person's character and spirit are formed mainly during adolescence and youth, with a correct educational program, one can develop entrepreneurial qualities and spirit and get familiar with entrepreneurial business. In this article, the definition and conceptualization of entrepreneurial management has been discussed.

Definition of entrepreneur and entrepreneurial management

The word "entrepreneurship" became common in the French language centuries ago and before it was mentioned in today's language. This word is equivalent to the French word Enterprendre, which means to undertake, equivalent to under Take in English, which was translated into Entrepreneurship in English by John Stuart Mill in 1848.

An entrepreneur is someone who undertakes to organize, manage, and assume the risks of an economic activity (Webster's Academic Dictionary).

An entrepreneur is someone who tries to make a profit by starting his own company or acting alone in the economic world, especially who must accept risks (Cambridge Dictionary).

In Encyclopaedia Britannica, an entrepreneur is defined as: a person who organizes and manages a business or economic institution and accepts the risks arising from it.

Joseph Schumpeter (economist) proposed that entrepreneurship involves innovations and untested technologies. He proposed creative destruction. It replaces products, processes, ideas and businesses with better ones. He believed that entrepreneurs are the driving forces behind active destruction.

According to Peter Drucker, entrepreneurship is about maximizing opportunities. Entrepreneurs identify these opportunities and act accordingly.

Entrepreneurship management is an academic academic field whose purpose is to teach the principles and basics of entrepreneurship to students. Also, in a general sense, it refers to the art and skill that business owners use to hunt environmental opportunities in the light of creative thinking.

Misconceptions of entrepreneurial management

Successful entrepreneurship requires only one big idea: The big idea is only part of success in entrepreneurship. Understanding the needs of different stages of the entrepreneurial process, using an organized method in order to expand the entrepreneurial business, and being able to handle the challenges of business management and entrepreneurship are the key elements for success.

Entrepreneurship is easy: You might think that entrepreneurship is easy because you follow your passions and are passionate about success. It requires commitment, decision (intention) and hard work. Entrepreneurs experience difficulties and continue despite the difficulties!!

Entrepreneurship is a risky bet: Entrepreneurship is a calculated risk. Successful entrepreneurship means avoiding unestimated risks or minimizing risks.

Entrepreneurship is found only in small businesses: Entrepreneurship is found in any size organization.

Small and entrepreneurial businesses are the same: Of course, there are differences between an entrepreneurial business and a small business. Small businesses are not necessarily entrepreneurial, creativity and looking for opportunities are necessary for entrepreneurship. Small businesses can grow and become entrepreneurial businesses. Of course, there are different opinions about the number of employees. For example, in another definition, a company with less than 500 personnel is considered a small business.

Major advantages of entrepreneurial management

Salary: You will definitely earn more than when you work for others.

Security: Continuation of personal business for several consecutive years also brings security during retirement.

Asset creation: As your company grows and becomes profitable, its value rises. Over time, the company becomes valuable.

Side benefits: such as a car for business purposes, short-term loan, life insurance, payment of entertainment expenses...

Independence: Your destiny is in your own hands. You are your own boss and employer. With the prosperity of your work, your financial worries will disappear.

Satisfaction: Excitement and challenges make your work exciting and bring you deep satisfaction.

Entrepreneurs mostly make decisions based on heuristic procedures. Managers check statistical information, credit, etc. and enable further growth in the future with their numerical budgets. Mere management is based on facts, but entrepreneurship is based on important beliefs and experiences. Entrepreneurs have mental leaps and do not always use a linear system of managerial thinking. Entrepreneurs make decisions in conditions of ambiguity and uncertainty. Making decisions based on reality sometimes makes facing a new opportunity costly and impossible. Entrepreneurship management will be a combination of these two categories and will raise organizational entrepreneurship.

Organizational entrepreneurship

Entrepreneurial management and organizational entrepreneurship should be distinguished. Entrepreneurship management is a broad scientific field, one of which is organizational entrepreneurship. In simple words, organizational entrepreneurship can be achieved in the shadow of entrepreneurial management. In order to better understand this category, it should be said that entrepreneurship is divided into two categories: individual (independent) and organizational. Organizational entrepreneurship is also based on innovation. The independent entrepreneur seeks to control the product market, but the organizational entrepreneur must overcome organizational issues in addition to the market. In an entrepreneurial organization, resources are more easily allocated to implement ideas.

In the entrepreneurial organization, quality is institutionalized in all dimensions. In this organization, there is self-selection and entrepreneurs do not wait for orders from above, supervisors also provide them with resources and time. Organizational entrepreneurship is a process in which innovative products or processes appear through the creation of an entrepreneurial culture in an organization. Organizational entrepreneurship relies on the resources and support of the organization. Innovation can be in the field of new products, organizational processes and management methods. In an entrepreneurial organization, everyone is an entrepreneur and the entrepreneur manager is at the top. While an organizational entrepreneur is someone who discovers and exploits new products, activities and technology under the support of an organization.

Knowledge Based Companies

Types of knowledge-based companies

To get to know the types of knowledge-based companies, it is necessary to say something about these types of companies. In general, knowledge-based companies are divided into two categories: manufacturing companies and start-up companies. In the continuation of this division, each of these main groups are also divided into two subgroups. In the continuation of this article, categories and types of division of knowledge-based companies will be examined.

Type 1 start-up knowledge-based company

Type one start-up knowledge-based companies refer to a group of companies that did not have a tax return for their last financial year or had no income in the last financial year. The expected product for this category of companies must have reached the production stage or at least be made to the level of a laboratory sample. In addition to having a design based on research and development, this product must have a very high level of technology and create a lot of added value in order to be included in the list of knowledge-based goods and services of the first level.

Knowledge-based and start-up type two company

The second type of new knowledge-based companies refers to a group of companies that do not have a tax return for the last financial year or have no income in the last financial year. . The expected product for this category of companies must have reached the production stage or at least be made to the level of a laboratory sample. In addition to having a design based on research and development, this product has a less sophisticated level of technology than type one start-up knowledge-based companies. The only difference between type 2 start-up knowledge-based companies and type 1 start-up knowledge-based companies is the lack of tax exemption, but they are completely equal in other benefits.

Knowledge base of commercialization

One of the most important issues and problems of knowledge-based companies is the commercialization of their brand and the sale of their products. The Presidential Office of Science and Technology has approved companies as knowledge-based commercialization companies by employing companies whose services are aimed at facilitating the activity and business development of knowledge-based or technological (non-knowledge-based) companies.

For this purpose, in the commercialization section of the list of knowledge-based goods and services, a section has been placed regarding companies that, with their services, promote the business of knowledge-based or technological companies, so that companies active in this field can obtain information about the existing and approved categories in the commercial sector and overcome this problem.

The definition of commercialization states: The transformation of new findings and research ideas into products, services and technologies that can be presented to the market. Commercialization can be defined as the entry of an idea or technology into the market.

Process and service based knowledge

Companies that produce non-knowledge-based products by using the equipment and processes mentioned in the regulations for the evaluation and recognition of knowledge-based companies, can receive type two (industrial) production knowledge-based approval. It is necessary to remember that the only difference between type two (industrial) production knowledge-based companies and type one production knowledge-based companies is only in not benefiting from tax exemption.

Soft and identity-building knowledge base

With the constant follow-up and support of the scientific vice president, a soft and identity-building staff was established in the scientific vice president and proceeded to compile the regulations in this area. Companies active in the field of soft technologies, like other knowledge-based companies, should have knowledge-based products with complex technology and high-level technology. Also, the financial, technical, and research and development features used in these companies are also examined. It is necessary to remember that the difference between knowledge-based production type two (industrial) companies and knowledge-based production type one companies is only in not benefiting from tax exemptions.

Basic knowledge of EPC field

The group of companies whose income is from the implementation of engineering, contracting and EPC construction projects, considering that at least 10% of the project includes knowledge-based criteria, can receive the knowledge-based manufacturing type two (industrial) certificate.

Essential financial skills for entrepreneurs

Entrepreneurial financial skills are one of the most critical prerequisites for starting and running a personal business. Since the success of any business is tied to providing expenses and making money, business owners should be able to handle financial affairs well. It does not make a difference in the essence of the story that you have taken the helm of which company in which field of work. In any case, the entrepreneur's financial skill will help you to develop your business faster while avoiding economic losses.

Understand the concept and importance of credit rating

One of the most important aspects of an entrepreneur's financial skill is having a correct understanding of the concept of credit and credit rating. The credit rating shows the eligibility of you and the collection under your management to use opportunities and financial facilities such as obtaining a loan. Banks, financial institutions, as well as real investors, do not want to provide their financial resources to people and businesses that do not have a proper credit rating because they consider such work to be financially risky. A credit score is a summary of how responsible you are for your financial obligations. Therefore, one of the basic requirements for the financial success of businesses, especially in terms of attracting capital, is having a high credit rating.

If you are stepping on the path of entrepreneurship for the first time and do not have much financial history, you should know that improving your credit rating will take some time and there is no way to speed up this process. Therefore, the best strategy is to continuously improve this rating by meeting current financial obligations and protect it against any threats that could cause it to decline. For this purpose, you should continuously review the payable bills to make sure that there are no delays or miscalculations in their settlement.

Spend your money wisely

Saving and frugal use of financial resources play a very important role in reducing business risks, and for this reason, you should pay special attention to this category as one of the most important aspects of an entrepreneur's financial skills. However, as important as it is to commit to a philosophy of frugality, you also need to be smart about identifying situations where you should spend money. One of the things that you should always prioritize for spending is the company and its requirements. This action can include buying new equipment or making changes in work processes with the aim of increasing the level of productivity. On the other hand, it is very important to pay attention to the needs of employees, especially their economic needs. There is a significant correlation between the satisfaction and satisfaction of employees, with the payment of adequate salaries and appropriate benefits to them. Satisfied employees show more hard work and commitment in doing their work, and this, in turn, leads to higher productivity for the company. Don't forget that offering more benefits to keep current employees is a logical move that will cost you much less financially than hiring new people. Therefore, do not underestimate the maintenance of economic satisfaction of employees in connection with the financial skill of the entrepreneur.

Be efficient in attracting financial resources

Attracting resources is one of the other important aspects of an entrepreneur's financial skills. Financial literacy is not just limited to capital management. Before managing the capital in his hand, an entrepreneur must have sufficient expertise in finding and securing it. You may need to attract financial resources for the company at the very beginning or sometimes in the middle of the work.

If you are just starting out, you should prepare a comprehensive business plan so that you can show it to potential investors and encourage them to participate economically in your business. This plan should be comprehensive, concise and useful and able to answer investors' doubts and questions well. Investors are usually highly intelligent and can correctly estimate the value and profitability of a business from its business plan, and they will not take a step until they are sure of the attractiveness of the project proposed to them! Of course, it should be like this. If you are an investor, before investing in a project, you will be looking for a logical and convincing reason to do so. Therefore, the entrepreneur's financial skill from this point of view has a high correlation with the quality of developing a business plan.

Borrow responsibly and with open eyes!

A manager who has the financial skills of an entrepreneur takes calculated loans to meet economic needs. If you are not interested in selling company shares to raise funds, there are other methods that you can consider, one of which is taking a loan. Most independent entrepreneurs cannot be successful in starting or running a business relying solely on their personal capital. For this reason, most of them consider taking a loan at different stages of the company's life as one of the ideal solutions for attracting the required capital.

You should start by looking at the loans you qualify for. If you, as a woman, intend to be an entrepreneur, you may be able to use the facilities specifically designed for women entrepreneurs. After choosing the best loan options, you should monitor the terms of receiving them as well as their repayment terms. Don't forget that your purpose of borrowing is to solve a problem and an ill-considered choice, you shouldn't turn borrowing into a complicated problem for your business!

What is the concept of marketing?

Marketing is a branch of management science that covers all stages of a business from product design to sales and has planning for it:

In marketing research, correct and principled ideas about product features are provided by accurate market needs assessment. In fact, in marketing, the customer who is going to buy the product is identified with all the individual characteristics and behaviors and habits, and the product is designed for a group of people with specific needs. After the production process is completed, the issue of introducing the product to the society and selling it, which is a part of marketing, is discussed. Also, one of the important points in the production of any type of product is branding, which is considered as a marketing topic. Considering the wide range of branches of this science, it can be considered as one of the most important sciences that is needed to start a business.

The definition of marketing from the perspective of Philip Kotler, the father of marketing science

Dr. Kotler is known as the father of modern marketing science in the world and has the most titles of management and marketing reference books in the world. He has published 34 volumes and more than a hundred articles in the field of marketing. Kotler's Marketing Principles book is still considered as the most reliable reference in marketing.

Philip Kotler defines marketing as:

Marketing is the science and art of finding, creating and delivering value to meet market needs with profitability. Marketing identifies unmet needs and wants. The market defines them and, by measuring the markets, determines its potential profit. Marketing identifies which segment of the market has the greatest potential to sell the product. (Actually, the product meets their needs) and designs and promotes the product or service accordingly.

Types of appropriate marketing in entrepreneurship

Viral Marketing

One of the common types of marketing in the world is viral marketing, which is an advertising strategy that uses the capabilities of social networks to promote a product.

The reason for choosing such a name for this type of marketing is to show the person who chooses this type of marketing that he can spread information about the product or other services in the community through social networks. Viral marketing is a type of information dissemination through word-of-mouth marketing strategy, but the modern technologies used in it allow its viral interpretation to include many Internet-based platforms.

Internet marketing

Internet marketing is a type of network marketing that is done through the Internet. This type of marketing is based on a set of electronic methods in the marketing process. Internet marketing can be considered as a branch of public recovery that has become famous among people in a very short period of time thanks to the modern technologies provided by the Internet. The types of internet marketing are:

1. Marketing through search engines
2. Content marketing
3. Types of social network marketing
4. Click marketing
5. Email marketing
6. Marketing through mobile apps

Drip marketing

Another type of marketing available to choose from is drip marketing. This type of marketing follows a communication strategy that sends a series of pre-written messages to your customers or potential buyers over time. These messages are often sent to customers via email. The types of drip marketing are:

1. Competitive drip marketing
2. Knowledge drip marketing
3. Basic drip marketing

What is marketing innovation?

Marketing innovation is the application of marketing management practices to create significant changes in product design, packaging, functionality, and performance. The combination of the two concepts of organizational innovation and marketing management does not fit in the field of innovation and is considered a blind spot for many researchers. Innovation in marketing does not think only about new product production, but includes all marketing processes and its goal is to achieve more profit. Marketing innovation means implementing a marketing method that includes significant changes in product design, product packaging, product positioning in the market, product promotion, and product pricing. The goal of marketing innovation is to better identify the needs of customers, open new markets or position the company's product in the market in order to increase the company's sales.

In fact, it can be assumed that marketing innovation leads to improved innovative performance. With the complexity of the competition, innovation is considered as one of the main advantages for the survival of companies. All air organizations need new and innovative ideas to survive. New and innovative ideas are breathed into the body of the organization like a spirit and save it from nothingness and annihilation. The emergence of innovation not only enables organizations to gain a competitive advantage over competitors, but also provides a useful tool to improve organizational performance. For organizations that compete in a variable and uncertain environment. Innovation (creating, transferring, reacting and changing creative ideas into action) is considered a vital factor for the growth, success and survival of the organization. In this article, marketing innovation is conceptualized and defined.

The concept of marketing innovation

Marketing innovation is the key to achieving differentiation in a repetitive business arena. Companies are trying to achieve this innovation by using innovation in traditional marketing mix as well as using new digital marketing methods. The result of these activities is that the business will have a recognizable difference among the competitors, which will improve the image of the organization with the customer. The characteristics of successful innovative and market-oriented activities include the appropriate marketing strategy, the path traveled in the market, the levels of management skills within the company and the unique organizational culture that may be difficult for competitors to imitate and copy. It is the specific combination of these factors that confirms whether a marketing innovation creates strategic value for the company or not?

Marketing factors can also be divided into four general areas that form the basis of marketing innovation. These levels are related to product, service, distribution, sales and promotion. Knowing these basic levels of marketing is essential; Because these factors are central to the company's marketing innovation; As a result, profit depends on value-added benefits within these levels. There is a general consensus on theoretical grounds that all types of innovation can contribute to competitive advantage and increase competitiveness.

The key to innovation in this customer-oriented approach is to achieve customer satisfaction.

The importance of marketing innovation

The effects of increasing innovation in organizations have caused organizations to consider innovation as one of the key factors in gaining a competitive advantage. The importance of innovation has caused the innovation-based perspective to be proposed as one of the four key perspectives of strategic management, the resource-based perspective, the industry-based perspective, and the organization-based perspective. In the model he presents, Kotler states that there is a relationship between the innovation-based perspective and three other perspectives (the resource-based perspective, the industry-based perspective, and the organization-based perspective) and the relationship between these four perspectives can help companies to increase their efforts to obtain a sustainable competitive advantage.

The subject of innovation, whether technological or non-technological, can improve the sustainable competitive advantage of the company. Innovation can be an important source of competitive advantage in the way of better performance. Innovation and competitive advantage processes are highly interdependent. A company needs to create new ideas to improve customer value and gain competitive advantage. Competitive advantage is created when the buyer receives the highest observed value in relation to other options (for example, a buyer from another source). (Arash Habibi)

How to identify the target market of your business?

One of the biggest marketing mistakes is to choose your target market too broadly. Attempting to attract any type of audience will cause your site's message to be lost. Business owners should define their target market to strengthen their marketing strategy. This issue makes you consider specific audiences for your business and work on attracting them. Understanding the motivations and desires of users will help you to offer them appropriate products and services. Understanding who you are going to serve is critical to the success of your business

What is the target market?

The target market is the audience that needs your products or services. These people are either your current customers or have the potential to become customers.

In order to properly market your products, you must first identify your target audience. If you are selling tractor parts, school teenagers will not be your target audience. Accurate definition of your audience is very effective in choosing your marketing campaigns.

Knowing your target audience is effective in choosing marketing methods. This issue can affect anything from content or activity in your social networks to connect your business directly to your target market.

Knowing the target market is actually knowing the characteristics of your target audience. But how to identify these features.

Take a look at your current customers

A good place to start is to review your existing customers. This can be the key to discovering the needs of your users. You can then focus your marketing strategies on these users.
As you work on your existing clients, ask yourself these questions:

What gender are the users most?-What is their age group?-Where do they live?-What is their profession?-What is their average income?-Do they have any common characteristics?

Once you have answered these questions, ask yourself how they will find you. The answer to this question can help you decide what you need to work on and what you don't need to work on.

Knowing your audience also helps the way you talk to them. This issue is very confusing when choosing the right marketing methods to attract them.

Rate your products and services

Analyzing your products and services will help you a lot while knowing your target market. Looking at the features of your products will create an image of their buyers in your mind.

Start by writing down the features of your products and then identify the benefit of each of these features. Think about everything your service or product provides.

After you write down the features of each of your products, determine who might be looking for it. For example, if you own an online hardware store, plumbers and contractors can be among your customers.

Put yourself in the shoes of the buyer

Create an imaginary persona of the customer according to the characteristics he probably has and that you have realized and put yourself in his place. By doing this, you will have a new look at your business and you will find out the things that need to be improved.

Whenever you put yourself in the customer's place, ask yourself why the customer needs your product and what is his motivation for buying? By being more specific on this issue and understanding the needs of users more and more, you will find out more about the general personality of your customers. Creating a fictional character and putting ourselves in his shoes helps us to become aware of real-life marketing opportunities.

Check out your competitors

After the initial definition of your target audience, you need to take a look at your competitors. Examining the marketing methods of your competitors and seeing the gaps in some cases can show you new ideas.

Search the Internet for keywords related to your business and find out the ways in which they are or are not working. Your competitors have the same target market as you. By looking at their products and the needs of their target users, you can see new products and new markets.

Don't be afraid to ask questions

Creating a survey on the website is a very good way to define the exact target market. These polls help you to learn more about the thoughts and motivations of users. When doing this, the most important thing is to determine what you are going to understand. Creating the right questions can go a long way in getting the right feedback.

Find out where users go first. Find out what motivates them to buy and find the person responsible for buying the home. Understanding the answers to such questions provides valuable information to understand the target market and reveals the reasons for the need for your services. You will also be informed of the first place that users go to when shopping.

There are many survey tools on the Internet that will help you create them. You can use these tools on your social networks or email customers after their purchase.

Use the power of social networks

Social networks have undoubtedly changed the methods of obtaining information. Platforms like Twitter and Instagram cannot be ignored by entrepreneurs and business owners.

In addition to finding new customers, you can also collect information with social networks. Social networks make the ways of communication with users smoother and we can use them to know the results of our activities.

Talk to customers

The most important reason for defining the target market in your business is to create a proper relationship with users. It's your audience that determines the type of marketing you do. For example, the target audience of a real institution is different from a coffee shop. Also, the style of preparing content, blog posts and social networks is also different for the audiences of these two businesses.

In order to establish a proper relationship with the target audience, it is necessary to talk to them in pleasant language. Use sentences that are familiar to them and that they understand.

5 new laws in the field of entrepreneurship and new product design

Joining the entrepreneurship and product design industry is like holding a baby and covering it. People are taught many rules and regulations during their studies and early days of work so that they can serve well in their jobs. However, in the last ten years, there have been major changes in the advertising, sales and marketing of pure entrepreneurial ideas and new product design.

The digital world is challenging old ways by embracing new ideas that lead the way in cutting costs. Therefore, the laws and guidelines of entrepreneurship and designing new products need to be updated and rewritten with the passage of time and a logical view. In order to adapt to the digital world in the field of entrepreneurship and designing new products, it is necessary to modify the 5 old laws and replace them with 5 new laws.

Old rule: Great work sells itself.

New rule: Great work needs sponsors and providers.

Perhaps many entrepreneurs, by designing and making a creative product, put their chest forward and think that their product will conquer the world. But due to the rapid growth of technology, entrepreneurs should no longer hope for the automatic advancement of their creative products. Every new product needs more than being creative, it needs good presentation and proper product support.

For example, Snapchat software is not suitable for a 55-year-old manager or a 14-year-old student. If the presentation and marketing of this software is not done correctly, responding to the disadvantages of this product for non-target audiences will be a problem for the credibility of its producers. Hence, a great business needs a proper presentation and good sales support to succeed.

The old rule: introduce and advertise the product in detail.

New rule: introduce and advertise the product in a general view.

This rule does not mean not to mention the benefits of the product; Rather, it means introducing the advantages of the product in the form of a brief but attractive advertisement. People in today's modern world have less time to pay attention to advertisements. Advertising on smartphones, billboards, tablets, leaflets, brochures or anywhere else is successful when it captures the audience's attention within a second or two.

The old rule: data is only for the accounting department.

New rule: Data is for all sectors.

In general, creative people are not interested in calculating numbers and consider this work as part of the duties of their accounting teams. They provide the data to the accounting team and receive only the interpretation of the data results from them.

But the fact is that this method was suitable for entrepreneurship and designing new products in the last thirty years. Currently, data plays a key role in the success of businesses, and data or information is considered a competitive advantage for companies against competitors.

Don't wait for the accounting team to get the results of your data interpretation, and do it yourself to identify useful data from non-useful ones.

If you pay more attention to details, you will find new and exciting directions for your creative ideas. Undoubtedly, data and information will dominate the advertising, design and marketing industries in the next few decades.

Learning the language of data is essential to achieving modern creativity. Learn this language so that you don't ignore pure ideas for entrepreneurship and designing new products.

The old rule: strive for rewards.

New rule: Strive for great results.

Many entrepreneurs and creative people strive to get gifts, awards and special badges and are eager to earn them. But doing things to win Oscars is not the pinnacle of success in entrepreneurship and product design.

It's time to put the thought of getting awards out of your mind and focus on doing a great job, getting feedback on the results from the client.

More awareness of customer opinions and demands leads to more sales and attracting them. The main goal is to achieve success through the customer and the best prize is to achieve excellent results and customer satisfaction.

The old rule: live to work.

New rule: work to live.

The advertising industry is proud to work with very hardworking employers. These people only take a few hours off on weekends or at least a few days a year. This way of working and living must change.

Having enough sleep or spending time with family and friends is a badge of honor. Entrepreneurship and designing new products is not necessarily the savior of your life, and it is not necessarily the cure for all the pains in the world. Entrepreneurship and designing new products is the only way to meet an important need and earn money to live a peaceful life.

What is e-commerce and what are its advantages and

disadvantages?

E-commerce was first introduced in the 1960s through an electronic data interchange (EDI) over value-added networks (VANs) and grew with the increased access to the Internet and the emergence of popular online retailers in the 1990s and early 2000s. For example, the Amazon website started in 1995 in Jeff Bezos' garage as a book shipping business. Or the EBay website, which enables online buying and selling between consumers, introduced online auctions to the world in 1995, and in 1997, with the great popularity of Beanie Babies, it became very famous and popular. With the increase in the number of Internet users, many believe that e-commerce will soon become the main way of conducting business transactions.

E-commerce, like any other digital technology or consumer-driven shopping market, has evolved over the years. As mobile devices become more popular, mobile phone business has also found its own market. With the emergence of sites like Facebook and Pinterest, social networks have become an important driver for e-commerce. For example, according to Paymill, since 2014, of sales made on Shopify's e-commerce platform that were driven by social media ads, 85 percent of shoppers were directed to the platform using Facebook ads.

The changing market provides a great opportunity for businesses to improve their customer relations and expand their market in the online world. According to Statista, by 2013, global e-commerce sales reached $1.2 trillion (1000 billion), and mobile phone sales in the United States reached $38 billion. More than 40% of Internet users (a total of 1 billion people) have purchased goods online. These figures will continue to grow as mobile phone and Internet usage continues to expand, both in the United States and in developing markets around the world.

Categories of e-commerce

☐ B2B (Business to Business) – involves companies doing business with each other. For example, manufacturers who sell their product to distributors and wholesalers who sell products to retailers.

☐ B2C (Business to Consumer) – includes businesses that sell goods to the general public through online stores without the need for any human interaction. This is the idea that most people have about "e-commerce". For example, we can refer to the Amazon online store.

☐ C2B (Consumer-to-Business) – In C2B e-commerce, consumers submit a project online with a specified budget, and companies bid on the project. Then the consumer checks the price offers and chooses the company he wants. The Elance website is an example of this type of e-commerce.

☐ C2C (Consumer to Consumer) – This type of business takes place in online classified ads, forums or marketplaces where people can buy and sell goods with each other. Craigslist, eBay, and Etsy are examples of this type of e-commerce.

Advantages of e-commerce

Advantages of e-commerce for customers

• Convenience

Any product you want is literally just a click away on the internet. Just type the name of the product you are looking for in your favorite search engine and all the options will appear in an organized and orderly way in just a few seconds.

•Saving time

With e-commerce, you no longer need to drive around for hours, browsing stores hoping to find what you want. Online stores offer you their full line of products and use warehouses instead of using stores to offer their products. You can find the products easily and they will arrive at your door within a few days.

• The existence of a wide range of different options

In e-commerce, a customer can easily compare products without having to go from one shop to another and find out which seller offers the best price and has more options to choose from. In the real world, every store has limited space, but the same store can offer the entire stock on the Internet.

• Comfort in comparison

In e-commerce, pair-by-pair comparisons are easy to do. When the goods are offered online, all their specifications and features are stated and the online stores want you to compare their goods with other goods so that you know that they offer the best options and come back to that store to buy again.

• Ease of finding reviews and opinions

Because the competition is so high, companies want you to look at the opinions and reviews of other consumers. There are positive and negative reviews on every website, and in addition to seeing positive reviews and comments about each product, you'll also get to know the reasons for those who didn't like that product.

• Coupons and discounts

There are tons of coupons and discounts for any online business you're looking for, and that's generally great for customers. With sites that act like department stores, you can find items that are up to 80% off! Make the most of this competition and find the best available price.

Disadvantages of e-commerce

Disadvantages of e-commerce for customers

• Privacy and security

Before making transactions online, first check the security certificates (such as electronic trust symbol, etc.) of that website. It is true that online shopping is easy and convenient, but no one likes to have their personal information stolen. Many sites are reliable, but again, you should always do your research and identify sites that are not secure enough.

•Quality

Even though in e-commerce, everything is readily available, the customer can only actually see and touch the products after receiving them. Therefore, before buying, you must check the method of returning the product if you are not satisfied with it. Always make sure there is a return option before purchasing.

• Hidden costs

At the time of purchase, the customer will be aware of the price of the product, the cost of transportation, loading and tax. But you need to be careful, because there may be hidden costs that are not mentioned on your purchase invoice, but appear on the payment form. There may be additional charges for handling and loading at the seller's location (especially for international purchases).

• Delay in receiving goods

Although in most cases, products are delivered faster than expected, you should be prepared for delays in receiving the goods.
For example, a snow storm at one point can disrupt the entire transportation system in the area. There is also the possibility that your product may be lost or delivered to the wrong address.

• Internet required

Using the internet is not free, and if you are using free Wi-Fi, there is a chance that your information will be stolen on an insecure website. If you don't want to use the free internet or you can't have internet or a computer at home, it's better to make your purchases in person.

• Lack of personal interaction

Even though the rules and regulations of every e-commerce business are made available for you to read, there is a lot to read and the legal issues can be confusing. For large or important orders, there is no one you can talk to face-to-face about your questions or concerns.

Disadvantages of e-commerce for businesses

•security issues

Although businesses take many steps to keep themselves and their customers safe, there are people who can break through any firewall and get the information they want. We have all seen in recent years that even the biggest and most famous businesses can be hacked.

• Payment and financial issues

Many financial institutions take the side of the customer when there is a bill payment dispute because they want to keep the customer. This issue causes damage to the e-commerce business when the goods have already been delivered to the customer, but the amount paid has been returned to the customer's account.

• The need to allocate more money for e-commerce infrastructure

It costs money to make sure your online business is run properly. As the owner of that business, you have to make sure that the transactions are done correctly and the products are displayed in the best way. To ensure this, you should hire a professional to fix the existing deficiencies.

• Referral of goods and after-sales services

Online business infrastructure must be complete and flawless. This also creates other costs for the business, because there are customers who are not satisfied with the quality of the product after receiving it and refer the product. In particular, there are consumers who want more than a refund.

• Availability of sufficient internet services

Nowadays, apparently all people can always use the Internet, but you should know that there are still areas where network bandwidth can become a problem. Before starting your e-commerce business, make sure that your area has the telecommunications bandwidth necessary to run your business effectively.

• Continuous maintenance

When a business starts e-commerce, it needs to be ready to change in order to stay relevant. As technology evolves, the systems used in your business must also be kept up-to-date or replaced as needed. Or there may be overhead costs to keep databases and software running.

What is a startup?

Although there is no emphasis in the definition of a startup that its activity must be in the field of technology or information technology, but because many startups have been formed in recent years around these fields, sometimes in the definition of a startup it is also mentioned that the startup should be active in the field of new technologies.

In this field, there is a difference of opinion whether every new activity should be considered a startup or not. In most academic books on entrepreneurship, even those that are more modern and innovative in their approach, start-up has a broad meaning and any nascent business is called a startup (e.g. Barringer's book on entrepreneurship).

But those who know the culture of Silicon Valley companies and follow the managers, consultants and theoreticians of technology companies, in their books, articles and interviews, consider a more limited meaning for startup and distinguish between startup (or start-up business) and small business (Small Business).

In most of the supplementary lessons, we separate startup and small business from each other, and if there is no such point of view, we will explicitly mention it.

Definition of a startup by the US Small Business Center (USSBA)

The USSBA defines startups as businesses that have two characteristics. First, they are usually formed around technology, and second, they have high growth potential.

This center emphasizes that the high growth potential makes startups worry about financing and seek to attract money more than non-startup small businesses. Because their founders usually believe that by attracting capital, they can quickly gain and take over a larger share of their potential market.

The main characteristics of startup types

In order to be able to consider a business in the category of startup businesses, it is important to examine the presence of several main characteristics of a startup in its main nature. Being new to a company does not necessarily mean that it is a startup. These are actually the features that all startups have in common.

1. Innovation

In order to achieve a sustainable competitive advantage that can guarantee the presence of this type of business in the market, innovation is an important feature. This innovation may exist in products or business model related to the company. Innovation plays an essential role in the success of a startup, so all entrepreneurs should consider this aspect seriously.

2. Age

A startup company is a company that is still in the early stages of brand management, sales and hiring employees. Most of the time, this concept is reserved for businesses that have been in the market for less than 3 years. However, this interpretation of a start-up company is not correct. You can have 7 years of experience in the company's work file and still be classified as a startup business.

3. Growth

The goal of a start-up business is to grow, expand and progress rapidly, and sometimes this growth manifests itself in extreme proportions. In simpler words, at a certain point of time, the growth that we normally and continuously consider for a startup company goes faster and more steeply. This line of growth in startup business is one of the points that make it stand out.

4. the danger

There are always several uncertainties about the complete success of a business. This means that in a business, you can never take an action where the risk or failure rate is definitely equal to zero. Startup companies are not exempted from this rule or are even more exposed to risk. For this reason, these businesses are considered high risk investments.

5. flexibility

A startup is very dynamic and ready to adapt to any problem that may arise. It must have the ability to meet the necessary needs to manufacture its products, in order to present them to customers. Also, to become a sustainable business; In different cases and sectors, include the ability to meet needs in its business characteristics.

6. solve a problem

Startup companies aim to solve the problem in the market and most of their activities are focused on this goal. So they focus on making a difference, not only in the market but also in people's lives, through product or service delivery.

7. comparability

Startup means a company that is constantly searching for a business model that is comparable and repeatable, that is, it can grow without the need to increase human or financial resources.

8. team work

This category of jobs usually consists of a small number of people. Nevertheless, teamwork and the commitment of all team members to the goals of the business and start-up business is one of the important parts that cannot be overlooked.

In short, in the answer to what is a startup, we can say that it is a company that is in the early stages of development, in order to solve real-life problems by providing an innovative product or service.

Should a startup business be done on the Internet?

The connection between these startup companies and technology comes from the 1990s, because these types of new business companies in Internet business formats have the ability to receive user experience feedback very quickly while users are using the product and use it to improve product development.

This is why internet businesses have a high ability to use startup models for development. Nevertheless, although many of the existing innovations are present in the field of technology in terms of nature, this does not mean that all types of startups are placed on the

Internet platform.

As we said, the types of startups are not only done on the Internet, but its types and categories are also an important part that we will address.

What does startup culture mean?

Organizational culture is important for all businesses, but it is critical for startups. Why? Because startups grow much faster than other businesses and require high team commitment, and the thing that can move these two together well is the same culture.

It is the culture that determines what decisions the team members make and how they feel about their work environment. What characteristics should this work culture have?

• Agility

In startups, the information and business process should flow continuously and without interruption, and each team member should know the organization's culture and hierarchy well and know what his duty is and what is expected of him.

• Multitasking

In startups, unlike large companies, the work team is small and there is not much hierarchy and its structure is flat. So, in such a structure, each team member should be able to do several tasks at the same time, even if it is outside of his area of expertise.

•team work

In the startup environment, people should be open to differences and they should look for different points of view and discuss them. Here, conflict can be good and constructive, provided that issues do not become personal and cooperation is based on trust and security. Team members should be available and reliable to others, ask each other for opinions and all of them participate in decisions.

• Enthusiasm and creativity

Most startups are basically formed based on these two factors, and research has shown that these two factors have a direct impact on the growth and success of any business. Interest in the creative idea is the primary factor that allows startup teams to work on an idea for long hours, without getting tired and without losing their motivation.

If you are an entrepreneur, check whether your work culture includes these 4 factors. If your answer is no, here are some ways you can build a better culture and help your business grow:

• Hire the right people

Since your team is so small in the beginning, the importance of having carefully selected forces increases because each of them can play an important role in shaping the work culture. Remember that the right person is not necessarily the one with the best resume. People's mental health and mindset, their motivations to work and their compatibility with other team members are more important than education and experience. Also, your team should include people with different ways of thinking because without different points of view, creativity and flexibility in your culture will decrease and you will not be able to understand the needs of different audiences.

• Define your values

Know what your values are from the very beginning of your career and convey them to the team members and ask them to tell you if these values prevail in the workplace or not. The amount of time you spend on each activity in your business shows your team what is truly valuable to your business.

• Recognize people's achievements

Many of your team members need this to stay motivated and energized, so recognize their successes to build a better culture. By doing this, your team members will feel valued and their productivity will increase. Be attentive to the needs of your employees, because they will care about your work as much as you care about them.

• Be clear in your communications

The small and flat structure of your business allows you to be completely direct and transparent in your communication and information transfer with each team member and keep them informed of work progress or roadblocks. Be a listening ear for issues and problems or comments and feedback, and arrange individual meetings with team members so everyone knows their voice is heard.

Types of startups

After clarifying the question of what a startup is, the steps of designing a startup business and the main characteristics of a startup, it is time to identify the different types of jobs offered in the field of startup activities. Due to the increase in demand in this market, it is necessary for future entrepreneurs to know that there are different types of startups and in which field they are ideal to enter and operate.

To learn more, it is enough to start reading a few books in the field of fledgling entrepreneurship and find more information about various types of startups by searching.

In fact, with a simple study, you will see that there is no clear and agreed framework for classifying all startups. Sometimes startups are divided based on the field of activity. Sometimes, the criterion is the architecture of startups, and they try to classify and analyze each startup based on their different positions in different spectrums.

Naturally, choosing the right category for startups depends on your goals and expectations and for what purpose you are doing this category.

Different types of startups

According to renowned Silicon Valley entrepreneur Steve Blank, there are 6 different types of startups:

Life-based startups

This type of startups are created by the entrepreneurs themselves, and based on that businesses and people who are interested in their work operate freely. Examples of these startups are freelancers or web designers.

Small business startups

They don't consider society and big goals and only seek to provide comfort and financial well-being for their family. Examples of these startup businesses are hair salons, grocery stores, bakeries, and other such cases.

Scalable startups

This type of startups is founded by entrepreneurs who believe from the beginning that they can change the world with their business idea.

Examples of these include:
Google
Uber
Facebook

Startups designed to sell quickly
These businesses are born after achieving positive results that attract their attention, with the aim of selling to large companies. This type of startup is very common in web and mobile solution development companies.

Start-up of large companies

In this category of businesses, goods or services are placed that are quickly known in the market and can be offered to the general public. However, due to market changes, renewal of user needs, competitive pressures, in this type of business, they tend to create and supply new products for new users in different markets.

Social startups

Finally, there are businesses whose entrepreneurs want to make a difference in society and create a better world. Therefore, the main goal is not to make a profit; Rather, it is more to help the society. An example is charities.

Venture capital in startups

Providing the necessary capital for start-up and entrepreneurial companies and businesses that are prone to jump and growth of value and of course a lot of risk is called venture capital.

Planning, the last step of starting a startup

So, the complete design of a startup, according to what we said, includes: choosing the type of business and designing the canvas of the business model, as well as macro and strategic planning of the startup.

Now it's time to talk about startup launch, which is the final stage of design and before the start of operation. Therefore, it can be viewed from the point of view of a project, the end stage of which is the preparation of the place, equipment and personnel to start providing service or production.

What are the reasons for startup failure?

All startups claim a new idea to meet people's needs. Founders spend a lot of time perfecting their product without showing it to the customer. This is what causes failure. Because startup founders don't talk to customers and don't get feedback from them about their products. (Saturday weekly)

5 things to do after your startup fails

The experience of failure is a process that will happen to many new businesses and especially to entrepreneurs who are going through their first business experiences. Almost 50% of small businesses fail in the first 4 years of their startup, because they are the founder's first experiences in the workplace.

Even if you start your business with a fantastic idea, have a strong dedicated team, and consider many possibilities, there will still be external factors beyond your control that, along with inexperience, can cause startup failure.

So note that the experience of failure may happen to many businesses, but what should be done after this failure? Should you just be disappointed and give up the work environment or should you learn from past experiences and return to business with more strength?

The following 5 steps can be useful in the continuation of your startup failure:

Analysis of failure experience

Analyzing startup failure is the first step any failed business should take, because taking such a process leads to results that are useful in starting other businesses. Keep in mind that the reasons for the failure of a business can be identified, and as a result, you can have a detailed review of your startup to identify the most important factors that led to the dismissal of your business.

Get your capital back

Many startup business owners are people who put all their assets or maximum capital into the business, so one of the most important approaches you should take after your startup fails is to collect your personal assets. Especially if you have invested a large percentage of your capital in a startup and the said business is going through a failure experience, think about consolidating and returning your assets very soon; Because you will definitely need it if you start a new business.

After your startup fails, join other entrepreneurs

When a business owner experiences failure, the feeling of loneliness and lack of success surrounds him and such a feeling will weaken him spiritually, which is why we suggest you to be with other entrepreneurs. Accompanying entrepreneurs who have a lot of experience and may have seen the failure of their startup, both creates a sense of empathy and provides the possibility to transfer experiences and education, and as a result, more ideas and solutions will be presented to you to deal with the problems in front of you.

Attending various events, connecting with entrepreneurs through social media or even introducing yourself to them can be effective in finding entrepreneurs who will help you through your failure experience.

Take time for yourself

Let's think more positively! An entrepreneur is very busy and 25% of them work 60 or more hours a week. One of the things you can do after your startup fails is to take time for yourself and rest.

Coping with the stress caused by failure and then starting a new business requires mental rest and peace, that's why it is better to take some time after the business failure, do the things you like, go on vacation, organize the housework, etc. to regain your lost mental and physical strength.

Thinking of a new business after a failed experience

Finally, the time will come to present a new program. After your startup failed, you investigated the reasons for failure, consulted with other entrepreneurs, took your time and raised your seed capital; Now it's time to present a new program.

If you have entered the commercial and business arena as an entrepreneur, no failure will definitely disappoint you, so go after your entrepreneurial dream and choose newer and more efficient ideas; Because you have definitely learned a lot from the experience of failure and it will be effective in your new business. (Fahima Khorasani, Saturday Magazine)

Examining solutions to overcome difficult situations

How do entrepreneurs overcome business problems?

Facing difficult situations is a natural thing in the business world. In any case, things will not always go as we predict. The important thing is not to despair. In fact, entrepreneurs should never give up. The best decision in facing unfortunate situations and bad events is to try to forget them and compensate through effort and effective work. Although forgetting the inappropriate events and focusing on the future is a very good idea, however, in such a situation, we should still think about measuring the amount of damage caused. Note that even if things don't improve after changing our business direction, the world is not over.

Be kind to yourself

The first step to regaining self-confidence and normalizing conditions is to accept a seemingly simple truth. That the situation is not always going to go according to our plan. Although this is very simple to say, it undoubtedly has its own difficulties in the implementation phase. That's why most entrepreneurs never pay attention to it. The prevailing practice among entrepreneurs is to try to find the culprit. In this way, others are always blamed for failures. When we accept the fact that the future is not always based on our plan, then we will focus on our mistakes instead of trying to find fault. The most important result of accepting mistakes is the ease in the process of finding our faults. In this way, it will be possible to prevent repeating mistakes.

Note that no matter what we do, failure and bitter incident will not be compensated, so instead of taking emotional actions, we should seek to find the causes of the problem and ways to prevent it.

Undoubtedly, trying to find the cause of accidents requires a lot of concentration and time. However, as an entrepreneur, we must also pay attention to our business. For this reason, there may not be enough time to find the root of the failures. The important thing is not to rush to find the root of the incidents. Except in the most critical cases, you have plenty of time to consider the various dimensions of the event in question. Therefore, my advice here is to keep calm and move things forward harmoniously.

Review strategies

Never let your ideas blind you in the world of entrepreneurship. If a strategy fails again and again, it means that it is not aligned with the business conditions and our company. Unfortunately, many entrepreneurs show great resistance to changing their ideas. That's why they will use any justification arguments against changing it. The important thing is to look fairly at our ideas. Based on this, even using other people's ideas will not be unreasonable. After all, maybe they have a better plan. Resistance to other people's interesting ideas is one of the main reasons for the failure of many start-up businesses.

Undoubtedly, different markets are constantly changing. Because of this, after a certain period of time, the program of brands will no longer respond to the changes that have occurred. For this reason, it seems necessary to review the strategies. Otherwise, there will be a possibility of repeating unfortunate events and successive failures. Fortunately, today, many agencies are active in the field of providing practical advice in various business fields. If rethinking your brand strategy seems difficult, go to one of these agencies. Of course, this option requires a suitable budget. If you are in a bad financial situation, start your own business. Today, the development of the Internet has made it very easy to access various sites in the field of business. In this way, you will become an expert in the field of business.

Pull yourself together and fight what happened

Successful brands usually present a powerful image of themselves. If we take a short look at the appearance of big brands, they all show a very elegant and at the same time specialized view of themselves. As an entrepreneur, under no circumstances should we lose our confidence. Many brands disappear from the business arena not because of bad performance, but because of the loss of their confidence and authority. In their personal life, many people face difficult problems and are under pressure for several months. It usually takes six months to a year to get over bad situations in one's personal life. Similarly, in business, overcoming problems takes time. In this way, discard the strange idea of improving the situation in the shortest possible time.

The best course of action after encountering an inappropriate event is to try to make a list of things that cause us problems in our work. In this way, during the process of improving our brand, we will also find the cause of failure. After we find a list of reasons for our failure as entrepreneurs (in larger cases, our brand), it's time to replace them. At this stage, we should seek to replace the causes of failure with more harmonious behaviors. In this way, at least we will not face a similar problem in the future.

A different look at obstacles

Maybe you tried to solve the problems facing your brand, but they disappeared as soon as you took action. Normally, many brands face this problem. Accordingly, when trying to solve the problem, the problem suddenly disappears. However, it will reappear after a while. In such cases, we have to change our approach. The best solution here is to get help from our friends. Choose one of your friends. Then share your views on the problems with him. If your view seems inappropriate and superficial to your friends, you should definitely look for a new and more practical solution. Usually, getting help from the same friends will be very effective to achieve a new approach. Otherwise, we should go for ideas from professional experts. Here again, we must have a suitable budget for cooperation with business agencies. Fortunately, in most cases, talking with friends or employees and the process of thinking together solves the problems, so put the option of cooperation with business agencies as a last resort.

Many brands have been in real chaos during their lifetime. However, their high self-confidence and the pursuit of proven solutions have saved them from difficult situations. If our business does not have suitable conditions, one or more reasons have created it. Undoubtedly, in such a situation, it will be difficult to find the root of the problems. However, finding them alone can put our brand back in good condition.

Do not believe in the concept of failure

Undoubtedly, failure is one of those words that does not deserve to be in the dictionary of our life. If you consider failure as the lowest possible point (in any case), it is likely that your business will end in failure. For this reason, according to many successful entrepreneurs, the concept of distance to success should be used instead of the concept of failure.

While strategies, money, plans and deals have an undeniable place in the success structure of any business, as an entrepreneur we must always set our mind on achieving our set goals. In this way, failure and loss of anything will never enter our mind.

Go back to your first point of view

Everything started at a certain time. Undoubtedly, all of us have been aware of the reason for our presence in the business world when we started working as entrepreneurs. In this way, we do our best to improve the situation. Unfortunately, in some cases, people and brands forget the main reason for their presence in the business world. Undoubtedly, such an event is not good news at all. For this reason, one should seek to restore the original goals. The best course of action in such situations is to try to remember why we are in the business world. This view will help us in the best possible way to overcome the problems.

Reasons why entrepreneurs fail in business

Do you want to start a new business but are afraid of failure? Next, I will tell you the main reason why entrepreneurs fail in business, along with ways to prevent them.

Every entrepreneur who takes the risk of starting a business has profit in the back of their mind. Owning a business can be very rewarding and at the same time very risky. There are certain factors that can be the reason for the failure of entrepreneurs in business, but the lack of proper and sufficient research on the profitability of the market before such a risky investment is one of the main reasons for failure in business.

Enthusiasm is the key to success in business, but it cannot guarantee profitability. If you're passionate about something but can't make money from it, and yet accept the risk of investing in it, then you're more like a philanthropist and social entrepreneur who wants to serve others with no or minimal profit.

Before accepting the risk and investing in any business, comprehensive research and consultation with experts is very appropriate and useful. No one wants to have a failing business. The pride of every entrepreneur is to witness the growth and sustainable profit of his business.

Some entrepreneurs start a business, but due to some special factors, their business fails after a short period of time. In the following, I will discuss some basic causes of business failure and the reason why entrepreneurs fail in business.

Lack of consultation from professionals

The first reason entrepreneurs fail in business is that they feel they don't need to think like or consult with others. It doesn't matter how knowledgeable you think you are, when you want to start a new line of business, it's best to seek advice from professionals. This will help you determine if this business is as profitable as you thought. Oftentimes, entrepreneurs start a business because they have seen a similar business being profitable for others. Yes, maybe such a business is profitable for others, but maybe there is a secret behind this success. Maybe this secret is related to the location, good customer service, knowing the right sources to supply raw materials, etc.

It is very necessary and helpful to have a mentor who will always stop you from making stupid mistakes. Another advantage of consulting with professionals is that you meet and talk with people who have run a similar business before, made mistakes, and learned ways to fix or avoid those mistakes.

For example, Bill Gates and Sir Richard Branson had mentors like Warren Buffett and Sir Freddie Laker. If they had advisors and coaches, why not you?

One of the best pieces of advice I can give anyone in business is to never stop learning; Not only should you learn about marketing in your industry, but also how to buy and sell products and services in other industries, and how to improve.

Lack of proper attention to the customer

Prioritizing and paying attention to the customer is very important. A business that has good service and attention to customers will surely progress. Good customer service keeps customers coming back, and returning customers makes them loyal. If you don't treat your customers very well, they will be drawn to your competitors. Learn how to show your customers that you value them. Always ask them about the quality of your product and offer discounts for their feedback (whether positive or negative). If you don't get close enough to the customer, if you treat them like other salespeople, they will only come to you when they have no other option but you. Not paying enough attention to the customer has destroyed many businesses. Your customer service department represents your brand.

Imitation of others

What works for Mr. A may not work for Mr. B. Many people enter a business or choose a particular business because they have seen others succeed in this business and think that if they do the same, they will be successful. It is better to consolidate this raw idea through appropriate consultations, and to recognize your points of difference and distinction compared to others. Imitation without consultation leads to a dead end. Never imitate, innovate.

Lack of experience

Lack of experience is another reason why entrepreneurs fail in business. If you are inexperienced or your management is raw and beginner, your business is doomed to fail. When starting a new business, it is recommended to use the services of experienced people in that field. They can be your partner or employee. Be sure to use experienced marketers and trained customer service employees.

Lack of accounting

You must account for every riyal that you earn in your business. Often times, many entrepreneurs do not keep track of their daily sales. When they sell one day, thinking that they can sell the same amount tomorrow, they spend their profit on their personal needs. If you want to succeed in your business, you must account for every rial of your income. Be sure to plan carefully for your expenses, because if you want your business to grow, 60% of your profit must go back to the business; In addition, you should leave one tenth of it as tax.

Lack of personal growth

Many entrepreneurs do not invest in themselves. They want to be good and successful, but they don't study, they don't research, and they don't attend seminars and workshops that will increase their level of knowledge. Personal development in the field of behavioral and communication skills is a necessity. Achieving this skill is difficult and requires discipline and precision. It is very difficult to achieve success without correcting and improving your behavior. No one has progressed in life without self-improvement and increasing their knowledge. Never stop learning.

Inappropriate location

An entrepreneur decided to establish a coffee shop in a local area. The coffees of that coffee shop were very pleasant and reasonably priced. His relationship with customers was also excellent. But after a year, his coffee shop did not grow enough and he could hardly manage it; So he decided to sell the coffee shop. After that, the 29-year-old entrepreneur, who also had enough capital, felt that he could make this business profitable and fashionable by injecting money into the coffee shop. He also failed to make this coffee shop profitable.

Why?

Due to the location of this business. The result is that you cannot start your business anywhere that does not need your services. Making your business stylish and trendy will not make people come to you and stay loyal to you. Before choosing a place to establish a business, you should check the area well in terms of the market.

lack of concentration

Entrepreneurs can easily get sidetracked by too many side hustles. Every time they focus on one side, their thinking power decreases. A good entrepreneur or businessman never loses his focus from important issues and priorities. But some people get caught up in obsessions and perfectionism in minor preoccupations that they can easily delegate to other people. The entrepreneur must learn to delegate some tasks to others. A person's short-sightedness is revealed when he is obsessed with quantity rather than quality. Being busy does not mean being productive and effective.

False expectations

Some new foundations (startups) think that as soon as they enter the business, money will rush to them without any effort or plan. This belief is another reason why entrepreneurs fail in business. Sometimes, only the entrepreneurs themselves are to blame for doing what they love and thinking they know more than others. As a result, it should be said that starting a successful business is not like running two hundred meters, but like a marathon. If you don't want to die in poverty or see your business fail, you have to work hard. Never expect a reward for something you haven't done.

Give up quickly

This is the most important reason why entrepreneurs fail in business. If you do not persevere; If you don't study and research; If you don't try again and again after a failure, you may not succeed in your business. First, you should know that reaching halfway in business never means success. Another problem that causes business closure at the very beginning is the lack of financing or lack of funds. Many entrepreneurs make the fatal mistake of starting their business with insufficient operating budget. The life of such businesses is not that long because their founders are easily disappointed and discouraged; Especially if they have to compete with strong people.

I recommend that, before starting any business, make this sentence the queen of your mind: "I will do everything (positive work) to achieve success"; And this sentence alone can be the beginning of your success. This way of thinking will help you think in a wider scope for your business. Try and try and try again.

References:

Dr. Farzad Tabatabai. Art of Life website

Negar Zia'i Young entrepreneur essay

Entrepreneurship and the age of technology in the third millennium book

Heshmat al-Maluk Amini, investigation of personality traits of creative girls aged 15-16, Tehran, Al-Zahra University, 1375.

Sternberg, 1989, quoted by: Betul Mohin Zaim, comparison of creativity and personality traits of first-year students (entry 78) of arts, humanities, engineering, and medicine at Tehran University.

Alan Budo, Creativity in Education, translated by Ali Khanzadeh, Chehar Publications, 1358.

E. Paul Torrance, creative talent and skills and ways to educate them, translated by Hasan Ghasemzadeh, New World Publishing House, 1375.

Afzal Al-Sadat Hosseini, Analysis of the nature of creativity and its cultivation methods, Tarbiat Modares doctoral thesis, 1376.

Gerrard quoted by: Afzal al-Sadat Hosseini, ex.

Gholamali Afrooz, "Creativity", Tahseh Magazine, No. 241, Association of Parents and Teachers.

Ormüller 1992, quoted by: Morteza Lagi, investigating the phenomenon of creativity in elementary school textbooks, investigating the effect of teaching creativity in elementary students and presenting models for education, PhD thesis, Tehran, University of Tehran, 2013.

Bowman and Rutter 1983, quoted by: Morteza Lagi, .

Layton, quoted by: Morteza Lagi,

Osborne, Mayer 1996, Burchard 1999, citing Morteza Lagi,

Zitlo, 2000, quoted by Morteza Lagi.

E. Paul Tornesbe quoted from the newspaper Ekhtaz

Gholamali Afrooz, "The role of self-confidence in the creativity of teenagers and young people", Takhteh Magazine, vol. 159.

J. F. Neller, Art and Science of Creativity, translated by Ali Asghar Madd, Shiraz, Shiraz University Press, 1369.

Ali Akbar Saif, Educational Psychology, Tehran, Aghaz, 1998.

Robert. L. Solo, Cognitive Psychology, translated by Farhad Maher, Tehran, Rushd, 1371.

Betol Mohin Zaim, comparison of the level of creativity and

personality traits of first-year students (entry 78) of the fields of art, humanities, engineering and research, University of Tehran, 1379.

Tahereh Fathi, investigation of the personality characteristics of art students of Tehran University, master's thesis, 1374.

The basics of management with an entrepreneurial approach. Author: Dr. Seyed Abbas Heydari

A. Peel, Torrance, creative talent and skills and ways of their education, translated by Hasan Ghasemzadeh, New World, 1375.

Betul Mohin Zaim, ex

Source: The article "Ways of Cultivating Creativity" - Prepared by: Dr. Mehrangiz Shua Kazemi - Marafet Magazine Number: 92 (special issue of educational sciences) Qabas.org

Stephen P. Robbins and David E. Di Sanzo. Management basics

Dr. Mohammad Ahmadpour Dariani- Entrepreneurship- Definitions- Patterns- Publisher of Pardis Company

Jalil Samad Aghaei- Entrepreneurial Organizations- Publisher of Public Management Education Center

Peter Drucker - a scientific field called creativity - translated by Seyyed Saleh Vahedi - Tadbir Magazine No. 43

Ali Nili Aram- Creativity and innovation in the organization of Tadbir Magazine No. 85

Taraz Am Amabayl - How to destroy creativity - Hossein Hosseini translator - Tadbir magazine

Dr. Seyed Mehdi Elwani - General Management - Ney Publishing

Hamshahri newspaper, Thursday, July 2, 2014, year 13, number 3730, page

Introduction to Entrepreneurship Management written by Milad Rabiei, Pars Electronic Publishing, Editor

House of Iranian entrepreneurs

success Journal

Online Economy on 23/06/2018

Fakher Holding website (Essential financial skills for entrepreneurs)

The specialized website of Pars Madir

Shabnam Jafarzadeh. Saturday weekly newspaper

The book of failures and success of entrepreneurs. Jacqueline Liana

https://tinet.ir/

managementstudyguide.com

https://www.entrepreneur.com/article/338543

https://www.entrepreneur.com/article/242327
https://www.cleverism.com/
https://keydifferences.com/difference-between-creativity-and-innovation.html
https://www.cleverism.com/18-best-idea-generation-techniques/
https://www.webconfs.com/1115/how-to-identify-your-target-market-profile-to-get-the-most-out-of-your-marketing/
https://www.thebalancecareers.com/advertising-4161818
https://www.businessnewsdaily.com/4872-what-is-e-commerce.html
http://www.enkivillage.com/e-commerce-advantages-and-disadvantages.html
https://www.sba.gov/category/types-businesses/high-growth-high-tech
https://www.noobpreneur.com/2019/02/22/6-things-entrepreneurs-do-to-keep-moving-when-things-go-tough/

WRITERS

Farshid Aramjoo   Elahe Tushe   Nima Taheri

aramjoofarshid@gmail.com   Elahe77tsh@gmail.com   nimaathr@gmail.com

www.ingramcontent.com/pod-product-compliance
Lightning Source LLC
Chambersburg PA
CBHW070901260726
48661CB00004B/1531